FENG SHUI

for the

CLASSROOM

FENG SHUI

for the

CLASSROOM

101 Easy-to-Use Ideas

RENÉE HEISS

Zephyr Press

Chicago

Library of Congress Cataloging-in-Publication Data
Is available from the Library of Congress.

Feng Shui for the Classroom
©2004 by E. Renée Heiss
Printed in the United States of America
ISBN: 1-56976-174-4

Illustrations: Brittany Pladek
Cover Design: Monica Baziuk
Interior Design: Monica Baziuk

Published by:
Zephyr Press
An imprint of Chicago Review Press, Inc.
814 North Franklin Street
Chicago, Illinois 60610
800-232-2187
www.zephyrpress.com

 Zephyr Press is a registered trademark of Chicago Review Press, Inc.

CONTENTS

To my husband, Doug, for his patience and understanding as I spent many hours in the preparation of this book.

■

To my children, Chelle, Kim, and Val, who are just beginning to see the wonderful world of feng shui.

■

To my Dad, who taught me independence and an appreciation for all that is new and different in life.

■

And to the memory of my Mom who, after working for many years at Princeton University Press, would have been so proud to see the publication of her daughter's first book.

ACKNOWLEDGMENTS

This book would not have been possible without the assistance of many helpful people. From acceptance to publication, my editor, Ronnie Durie, was extremely patient with me as I learned how the pages combined to become a finished product.

When I learned that I needed to supply my own pictures for the book, I panicked. I'm neither a photographer nor a graphic artist, I thought, I'm a writer. So, I set off in search of both. Therefore, I extend a hearty "thank you" to the teachers at Springfield Elementary School, especially Eleanor Dunker and Sharon Downey-Hohmuth. Their dedication to feng shui in their classrooms has helped to produce the beautiful photographs of children enjoying their learning environments.

The artist, Brittany Pladek, was in my child care class the year I wrote the text for this book. As a senior interested in a journalism career, she is also a talented artist. Her drawings of "Ms. Chi" add the perfect touch of whimsy to my book.

Finally, my undying gratitude goes to Jessica Platt and Clay Giles. Two young lawyers, one of whom is the daughter of a friend of mine, graciously agreed to look over the publishing contract. Without their help, I would have been hopelessly mired in legal terms and never would have progressed to actually writing this book.

FOREWORD

What "Imagineers" created for Disneyland, Renée Heiss has done for educators. In *Feng Shui for the Classroom*, she lays the groundwork for how classrooms can be transformed to create powerful, inviting places to learn and grow. She has done so in a simple, straightforward, and very entertaining manner. Many researchers and practitioners have examined the effect "place" has on building and shaping our learning.

Modern science is confirming that our actions, thoughts, and feelings are indeed shaped not just by our genes, neurochemistry, history, and relationships but also by our surroundings. Some of the most intriguing findings dealing with the development of meaningful learning experiences focus upon the essence of place. In *The Experience of Place*, author Tony Hiss (1990) states,

> *We all react, consciously and unconsciously, to the places where we live and work. Ever-accelerating changes in our day-to-day circumstances are forcing us to learn that our surroundings, built and natural alike, have an immediate and continuing effect on the way we feel and act. In short, the places where we spend our time affect the people we are and can become.*

The implications for schools and classrooms are tremendous. If educators could understand the effect "place" has upon learning, much could be done to enhance the quantity of meaningful educational experiences. Understanding the feng shui of a classroom, the effect of color, temperature, smell, sound, over-stimulation, under-stimulation, and a host of other conditions, could dramatically impact learning. Our brains are so adapted to make associations with our environment that whether we want to or not, we link our experiences with their settings, and those two things together produce our behavior. We are now beginning to see that whenever we make changes in our surroundings, we can all too easily shortchange ourselves, by cutting ourselves off from some of the sights, sounds, shapes, textures, or other information from places that have helped mold our understanding and are necessary for us to grow and thrive.

In *Feng Shui for the Classroom*, the Chinese practice of feng shui is masterfully woven into the day-to-day operations of classroom teachers. While not easy to translate into Western terms, feng shui corresponds to what we call ambiance or a place's distinctive atmosphere. Feng shui combines bits of art, geophysical observation, psychology, religion, folklore, and plain common sense. It incorporates many of the insights from researchers on the link between our internal states and our external environments. The feng shui of a place is the quality that strikes you as soon as you enter. Balance, harmony, and flow are essential to positive feng shui. A place with good feng shui is neither boring nor agitating but promotes the right level of energy for the business at hand.

The underlying concept that has importance to educators is that living, working, and learning in harmony with the right classroom environment makes sense and can improve the quality and meaningfulness of one's education. Producing meaningful learning experiences requires that attention not only be given to the individual and the subject at hand but also to the character of a place, its essential spirit, livability, flavor, feeling, essence, presence, harmony, charm, quality, and its optimum level of feng shui.

The basic principle that links our place with our learning is simple: a good or bad environment promotes good or bad memories, which in turn inclines us to good or bad behavior. The principles of feng shui can help the classroom teacher create the most optimum learning environment possible. For many, the creation of a unique educational classroom or setting is more than just a passing whim or fancy. It is the result of thought, inspiration, integration of knowledge and information into action, and the realization that such designs present a living testament to feng shui. The challenge to those wishing to become more "feng shui literate" is to connect to the visual messages that exist within the walls of their classrooms, and see how the information shared by Renée Heiss has personal merit to them and their students. Her sections on "Classroom Decluttering" and "Classroom Design Elements" are especially powerful in terms of inviting real change to occur.

Feng shui in the classroom is often like an Alexandrian acrostic. Whether the message is read forward or backward, it still reveals the same thing: the significance, importance, and purpose of classroom design, and the "educational ecology" that is established, can have profound influence on the quality of teaching and learning. I applaud Renée Heiss in her efforts in bringing the message of feng shui out from the vocabulary of architects and "New Agers" to the real world of teachers. Through the understanding and implementation of the elements of feng shui, teachers are invited to create classrooms of trust, respect, optimism, and meaningful learning.

—PRENT KLAG, ED.D.
Department Chair,
Teacher Education
Southern Utah University
Cedar City, Utah
June 2003

FENG SHUI

for the

CLASSROOM

MY STORY

Teaching is a progression of actions and reactions. For ten years, I had taught Family Consumer Sciences—child development, fashion, and interior design. Then, six years ago, my district asked me to use my elementary certificate to teach two reading classes. With my certificate in order and my wits firmly planted where I would never find them again, I accepted the challenge.

One class had an average seventh grade mix of students. The other class, however, took most of my prep time and energy to keep it focused and on task. That class provided me with the insight that feng shui works in a classroom just as well as it works in a living room or corporate board room.

After feng shui adjustments, students tend to work diligently.

Sometimes There Are a Few Surprises in Teaching . . .

My language arts curriculum focused on creative writing. The school's reading teachers covered the literature; I had to get those students to produce. They didn't want to sit still long enough to listen to the assignment, let alone actually write several sentences with a cohesive link. I tried every model of reinforcement in the library, both positive and negative. Very little could penetrate their minds, which were filled with thoughts of problems at home, problems with friends, and problems with just being twelve years old. To say this class presented a challenge would be a gross understatement. And did I mention I had these individuals right after lunch?

I needed to summon a creative approach. My first success came sometime during the second marking period when I began to have "quiet time" before a focused writing assignment. I turned out the lights. I played both Mozart and New Age music. The students put their heads on the desks. I talked slowly and quietly about the task at hand. I let them think, sometimes snore, until I was ready to release them to pen and paper. Only five or six minutes of this saved the other thirty-five minutes from disaster. Following this meditative posture, I turned on only half of the lights and they went immediately to work. Surprisingly, most students finished the assignment with time to spare. Even more surprisingly, their essays were clear and focused. Their spelling left a little to be desired, but I left that lesson for another day. That first day, with the low lights, soft music, and gentle meditation, was a resounding success. The students actually began to *request* the guided essays.

Sometimes You Build on Past Experience . . .

Many disciplines are interrelated. My preparation in child development led me to see the relationship between my new tactics in the language class and Frederick LeBoyer's method of delivering babies, which he introduced in his 1975 book, *Birth Without Violence*. LeBoyer knew that babies didn't want to be born into a cold, bright, noisy world. I knew that students didn't want to leave lunchtime friends and be delivered to the hands of a language arts teacher. The French obstetrician's method stressed a calm, inviting atmosphere to produce a calm, endearing baby. This analogy worked for me. I looked elsewhere for other analogies, settled on my interior design curriculum, and found feng shui.

◉ Feng Shui Outside the Classroom

Convincing evidence for the benefits of feng shui can be seen in offices, homes, and even shopping malls. The Chase Manhattan Merchant Bank in Hong Kong struggled to build a firm financial base until corporate leaders employed a feng shui expert. Business picked up considerably once feng shui remedies were introduced (Too 1998). In 1971, after consulting a feng shui

A large part of the work of teaching is constructing the laboratory for learning: It must be sufficiently broad and varied to challenge a range of interests and abilities, and yet focused enough to offer students some coherent rhythms and goals (Ayers 1993, 50).

master, the Singapore Hyatt Regency hotel clientele proclaimed a marked increase in visual appeal, which in turn increased sales. Among other simple changes, the master recommended the addition of a fountain outside of the main entrance (Finster-Bytner Web site). Even financial mogul Donald Trump consulted a feng shui master to ensure his continued prosperity as he began work on the Trump Tower in New York City (Lagatree 1998).

Go into your favorite Chinese restaurant. Chances are you will see feng shui clues throughout the room. Fish tanks, red tassels, mirrors, and octagonal tables are all recommended by feng shui practitioners to improve business, provided they are placed in the approved quadrant of the room.

In 1992, a California builder was unable to sell one-third of his half-million dollar homes built in an upscale neighborhood. A feng shui expert suggested restructuring the straight walkways into curved ones and rectangular yards into arched, almost sculpted arrangements. According to *Fortune* magazine, the homes sold within three months (Kirsch 1992).

In a classroom, curves are more beneficial and easier to accept than straight lines. When students are placed in neat rows, the janitor's job may be easier, but teachers need to be able to circulate freely around student desks (Jones 2000). Why, then, do teachers continue to place students in neat rows at right angles to each other?

Why, too, have schools been excluded from the loop of feng shui success? Have administrators and lawmakers been so busy focusing on standardized tests, curricular requirements, and budget restrictions that they have been unable to see that a solution to learning problems, school violence, and financial setbacks

When students sit in rows, the arrangement discourages interaction. Is that what you truly want in a classroom—twenty-five passive, immobile learners?

could be well within their reach? Perhaps they need clear models to follow so they will see that feng shui is indeed a circuitous path that will terminate at high student achievement.

◉ Feng Shui in the Classroom

Feng shui softens the impact of the educational environment. Teachers and students spend one-third of their day in school, one-third at home, and one-third asleep. If the sleep time is eliminated, that leaves half of their waking hours in a place that could quite possibly be cluttered, poorly arranged, and, in short, not very comfortable. Psychologists recommend that a good house cleaning can help an emotional illness. A good classroom cleaning will have the same effect on the students and their teacher. Feng shui goes beyond classroom cleaning and into a new dimension of classroom organization.

When students are in harmony with nature, they feel comfortable with themselves. When they feel welcomed by a classroom's ambiance, they enter eager to learn. However, when they are greeted with a hodgepodge of supplies, desks, filing cabinets, books, worktables, and a teacher's cluttered desk, they feel repelled and depressed by those working conditions.

By using a common sense approach to feng shui in the classroom, you can increase your comfort factor. Think about your attitude as you walk into work each morning. Think about how you prepare for the day's lessons. Think about why you decided to become a teacher in the first place. Now think about how

comfortable you are right now with your decision to become a teacher. Which of the five comfort factors fits your current teaching situation?

C5 Most of the time, my students and I cooperate in a relaxed environment. Learning is fun for me and for them.

C4 I like my job as a teacher, but something just doesn't feel right in my classroom. I look around and everything appears to be in place, but I just can't pinpoint the problem.

C3 Some days are good, but most of the time I struggle for my students' attention. I wish I could find some new ways to get them interested.

C2 If I could only get these students to sit down, be quiet, and listen, I'd be able to accomplish my goals and objectives.

C1 I really need to find a new profession. I'm not happy at all.

Where are you in the comfort zone? If you are caught in C1 through C4, you probably need a feng shui adjustment in your room. If you are a C5, you are either already aware of the benefits of feng shui, or you have a natural talent for arranging your room in a pleasant, orderly manner.

Finally, consider the rising statistics on school violence. Video cameras, metal detectors, and code-activated locks have become accepted practice in a world where violence in school is far too common. Certainly, some students carry with them problems that begin at home. However, problems do not need to escalate at school. By arranging a classroom so that it is in harmony with the natural forces, teachers will be able to harness children's natural energies into a productive avenue toward educational success.

◉ The Rest of My Story

After those initial baby steps into more effective classroom organization, I began to reorganize subsequent classrooms. I read many feng shui books and watched feng shui videos. I looked at the symbolism and location of objects in my room. I incorporated feng shui lessons into my interior design classes. My students tried feng shui in their own homes and came back with remarkable stories of higher grades and better relationships with parents. Part of the success was probably due to the mandatory clutter reduction for effective feng shui.

I have since left teaching language arts and am back teaching Family Consumer Sciences full time. My classroom is feng shui compatible as I look to energize each area of the room. A frog wind chime graces my doorway and plants by the window draw energy from the sun. My classes are filled with eager learners who are generally polite to each other. Even the substitutes provide positive feedback, telling me it's the room, not the teacher, that is creating the difference.

Current research supports the effective use of environment in education. A 1999 study by the California Board for Energy Efficiency concluded that the size and location of windows

> The underlying important concept for educators is that living and working in harmony with your environment makes sense and can improve your life (Klag 1995, 6).

directly affects student performance. Feng shui masters would embrace that concept. Dr. Prent Klag of Southern Utah University has spent years investigating how to make schools "the most inviting place in town." In an e-mail interview, he declared that he is "more convinced than ever that the power of place is a major factor in meaningful learning." He is even so bold as to say that schools should use feng shui models to create a comfortable learning environment.

Feng shui works in my classes. Now learn how it can work in yours.

Watch your students carefully as they come into your room. Do they appear eager to learn, walking straight, their eyes directed into the room? Are any slumped with eyes downcast, wandering into yet another classroom? Perhaps some are distracted, walking backward as they finish a conversation with a friend? Do any appear to fear your class and the possible detention? Hopefully none of your students appears hostile, filled with hate for your class.

Tally your students for a week to identify a trend. Using the headings listed here, you may choose to analyze each student individually, each class (if you are in a middle or high school), or your classes as a whole. Hold on to this tally until after you are finished making feng shui changes, then tally again. You will be amazed at the difference in your totals.

EAGER	APATHETIC	DISTRACTED	FEARFUL	HOPEFUL

WHAT IS FENG SHUI?

Feng shui, pronounced *fung shway*, is the ancient Chinese method of design for balance and harmony. It is the arrangement of a room so that it agrees with nature. Just as the old commercial warned us not to "fool with Mother Nature," so too should we embrace, not reject, Mother Nature as she enters our classrooms. When Western designers and architects were busying themselves with line, form, function, and balance, Eastern geomancers had long since determined that when the earth's elements are placed in a pleasing manner, all goes well for those who live or work in that structure.

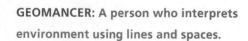

◎ How Did Feng Shui Begin?

Over three thousand years ago, farmers in southern China determined that crops grew better when placed on the southern side of their property. The wind (feng) and water (shui) there were very favorable for growing rice. These ancient farmers envisioned an energy (chi) that swirled about their crops, nourishing them with life-giving water and gentle breezes. On the north side of the land, however, harsh winds blew from the Gobi Desert. Sand blasted the crops and monsoon rains beat the crops down until the farmers had barely enough food for their families and none to take to market. The feng shui on the north side of the land was very poor. Since prosperity was related to crop success, facing south became desirable for other activities, such as the placement of the house. Warm sun filtered in through the front door of the huts, giving the family a feeling of togetherness and support from nature. Facing south became synonymous with good fortune (Skinner 2001).

In the early days, feng shui practitioners used the lay of the land to assign shapes and colors to their homes. The south, with its warming sun, was assigned the triangle and red color. The north, from which came the monsoon rains, was assigned a wavy shape and dark blue. The west, where the Mongolian mines produced ores, was assigned circles and white. (You might question the circle for the metal, but the ancient Chinese saw the beads of condensation that formed on the metal and, since circles were not assigned anywhere else, decided it would be a good shape to symbolize the metal element.) The east, with its wooded mountains, was assigned a rectangle and the color green. Finally, the center of the ancient Chinese world was labeled the earth and carried the square, a symbol of their garden plots. Many colors signified the earth—the yellow, pink, and turquoise of rocks and gems, and the orange, earthy tones of the soil (Too 1998).

◉ The Trinity of Luck

The ancient Chinese believed that three forms of luck influence all of us: Heaven Luck, Man Luck, and Earth Luck.

Heaven Luck is our destiny, dependent upon the place and time we were born. It affects about 40 percent of our lives. Obviously, we cannot change this part.

Man Luck affects about 25 percent of our lives. It is what happens through the normal course of our lives. Man Luck is controlled by everyday circumstances. Man luck is also controlled by the decisions we make in response to those everyday circumstances.

Earth Luck affects the remaining 35 percent of our lives. Earth Luck is where feng shui comes in. It happens as we manipulate our environment in order to harness the energy or forces of nature. By using feng shui principles, we can enhance the helpful parts granted by Heaven Luck and reduce the negative that happens when we misuse Man Luck (Too 1998).

◉ Western Feng Shui

Certainly, we do not all live in China, nor do we have western metals and eastern forests, but there is a certain comfort in

MAP OF CHINA

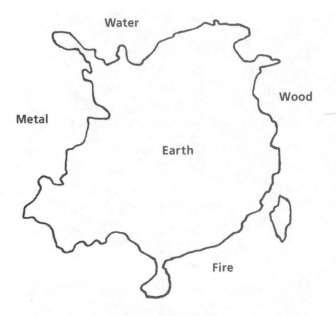

Water

Wood

Metal

Earth

Fire

Although feng shui principles were known for thousands of years, they were not formally written until the Han Dynasty in 25 A.D.

The only way to predict the future is to create it.

—Sign outside the gate to Great Lakes Naval Training Center, Illinois

knowing that all of the earth's systems can be packaged into five containers. Western feng shui is less oriented to the magnetic compass. It is more oriented toward placement of the elements according to the main entrance to a room.

By organizing our world according to these five elements, instead of dropping our belongings in a haphazard method along the way, we gain respect for our surroundings. It naturally follows that with respect for our surroundings comes respect for ourselves and those around us. Feng shui teaches respect, organization, and clarity of thinking that is necessary in modern classrooms.

Feng shui is not a religion, nor does it preach any religious tenets. It predates Taoism, Confucianism, and even Buddhism. The First Amendment Center, which works to preserve and protect First Amendment freedoms through information and education, has approved the organizational tips embodied by feng shui. Feng shui does not infringe upon anyone's freedom of religion.

Feng shui teaches a method of organization and appreciation for harmony. It helps people to become balanced in their environment and within themselves. True feng shui is a complex association of astral tables, magnetic pull, and environmental organization. After many years of study and practice, you would be able to tightly control your classroom using all of the concepts that feng shui embodies. However, you're busy. You plan, you implement, you organize, you grade, and you care about the children you see every day. Feng shui will help ease your burden by organizing your classroom into an easy arrangement of students, supplies, and furniture.

The concepts contained in this book will help you to understand the basics of feng shui as they apply to your classroom. Even using one or two suggestions will make an immediate improvement in your teaching environment. Learn how you can implement feng shui in your classroom so you can experience the success I found when I first tried some of the remedies.

◉ Find Your Best Direction

The following chart is based on a formula for finding your best direction (Too 1998). It also includes birth years so you can choose the best direction and location of your desk. The first direction is "best," the second is "personal growth," the third is "health," and the last is "romance." (You can decide what you want to do with the romance information!)

This formula supports the theory that students should not be placed in rows, as it would be physically impossible to arrange all of them facing their optimal direction. However, you need to remember that there are two ways of looking at this chart. One in which you bring a compass to school and locate magnetic north, then arrange your students accordingly. The other is part of Western feng shui, which will be explained in more detail later. In that arrangement, the door to your classroom is always north, the far wall is south, the right wall is west (looking from the door to the far wall), and the left wall is east. I find it easier to place students using the Western method, however, I have encountered students who were uncomfortable in the assigned

Feng shui has been credited with doing all manner of miraculous things, but what it is really best at is freeing up energy, increasing your luck, making many more opportunities arise, and/or making you more able to grasp them (Skinner 2001, 32).

position, and when I moved them to their magnetic comfort seat, felt better about their locations.

Note, also, that there are two basic configurations. One is considered to be an "east group" and these people should face E, S, SE, or N. The other is a "west group" and those people should face W, NW, NE, or SW. Generally, east group people get along better with other east group people, and the corresponding relationship occurs with west group people.

This might appear to be a seating chart nightmare, but if you label sticky notes with each student's name, best direction, and group, you will be able to rearrange them easily on your basic room chart.

BIRTH YEAR	DIRECTIONS FOR BOYS	DIRECTIONS FOR GIRLS
1940, 1949, 1958, 1967, 1976, 1985, 1994, 2003, 2012, 2021	W, NW, NE, SW	E, S, SE, N
1941, 1950, 1959, 1968, 1977, 1986, 1995, 2004, 2013, 2022	NE, SW, W, NW	SE, N, E, S
1942, 1951, 1960, 1969, 1978, 1987, 1996, 2005, 2014, 2023	N, SE, S, E	NE, SW, W, NW
1943, 1952, 1961, 1970, 1979, 1988, 1997, 2006, 2015, 2024	S, E, N, SE	S, E, N, SE
1944, 1953, 1962, 1971, 1980, 1989, 1998, 2007, 2016, 2025	NE, SW, W, NW	N, SE, S, E
1945, 1954, 1963, 1972, 1981, 1990, 1999, 2008, 2017, 2026	SE, N, E, S	SW, NE, NW, W
1946, 1955, 1964, 1973, 1982, 1991, 2000, 2009, 2018, 2027	E, S, SE, N	W, NW, NE, SW
1947, 1956, 1965, 1974, 1983, 1992, 2001, 2010, 2019, 2028	SW, NE, NW, W	NW, W, SW, NE
1948, 1957, 1966, 1975, 1984, 1993, 2002, 2011, 2020, 2029	NW, W, SW, NE	SW, NE, NW, W

✳ TRY THIS

Most people feel more comfortable facing a specific compass direction. Mine is east, with a secondary direction of south, which corresponds to the birth chart.

Using a compass, record where you choose to sit when all directions are available—at a restaurant, at your kitchen table, in your living room. Now try sitting at another seat and compare your feelings. Are you uncomfortable, anxious to sit at your "regular" seat? Or do you feel more relaxed? If the latter is the case, then you haven't been sitting in your optimal direction.

Now look at where you sit in relationship to the main door into each room. This is the method for finding your best direction according to Western feng shui. Do you generally sit facing the same direction? Most people find this to be the case.

Now consider this for your students. Arrange them by birth year as it relates to compass direction or the Western door orientation and notice a difference in their comfort factor.

SAMPLE ROOM ARRANGEMENT

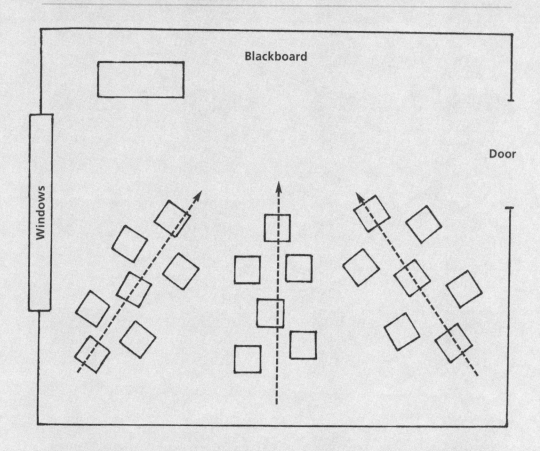

This arrangement allows for the flexibility to seat most students according to their best feng shui direction while facing the front of the room.

3

ENER-CHI EFFICIENCY

Think about when you feel most comfortable. You walk outside of your door—are you greeted with an arctic blast, or a warm breeze? You plan a trip to the ocean—are the waves crashing onto the rocks, or gently rolling in toward the shore? You stroll down a wooded lane—do airplanes screech overhead, or do the birds chirp? You go on a fishing trip—is the lake stagnant and putrid, or clean and fresh?

No matter how much you enjoy the rugged life, I'm sure you will agree that warm breezes, gentle waves, merry little chickadees, and fresh lakes present a more comfortable environment than arctic blasts, crashing waves, screeching airplanes, and fetid lakes. According to the ancient Chinese, the "chi" is better.

Chi is the elemental force that travels around our environment, both inside and outside our enclosures. (It is sometimes written Ch'i.)

Chi is the life force present in animals, the environment, the weather, and celestial configurations. It is a powerful force that can guide human beings in many directions. Conversely, people have the power to direct the chi in ways that increase or decrease the comfort in their lives (Lagatree 1998).

Feng shui creates environments in which the chi flows easily, swirling around our homes, offices, schools, and even our bodies to create a feeling of well-being. When we allow chi to move too quickly, like the crashing waves, or become stagnant, like the fetid lake, our environment and ultimately our health suffers.

When the chi flows gently through our gardens, the plants flourish. When chi becomes stuck in a myriad of weeds, the gardens become choked and slowly deteriorate (Hale 2001).

Why not carry that same logic to classrooms? When chi becomes trapped or speeds through the room, student interest withers. Students become lethargic and disinterested, or worse, they become arrogant and angry. When chi travels freely around the desks, students flourish. They are cooperative and eager learners.

The Nature of Chi

Three kinds of chi control our world: sheng chi (the good, motivating chi), shar chi (the overly fast, destructive chi), and ssu chi (the trapped, decaying chi) (Skinner 2001). For clarity, the chi referenced in this book always refers to the sheng chi.

Chi has four basic characteristics that control its influence over our environment: chi moves, it connects, it accumulates, and it desires change (Collins 1996).

Chi Moves

Remember, feng shui means wind and water. Chi moves just as wind and water, only it is a movement of energy rather than a physical movement. Wind and water become turbulent when they encounter obstacles in their path. Chi also becomes turbulent, but in a way that affects our health, wealth, relationships, and general composure.

At the Hotel Monaco in Washington, D.C., the decorators were confronted with extremely long hallways. The designer, Cheryl Rowley of Beverly Hills, California, placed side curtains at regular intervals to break up the speed of the chi as it traversed past the guests' doorways.

When chi is stopped by a poor arrangement of furniture, people become unbalanced and have a strong desire to leave that room. In a classroom, if the furniture is poorly arranged, the students will not feel welcomed. When chi travels too quickly through a room, people become eager to leave. In a classroom, the students will want to leave as soon as they enter.

How do you encourage chi to meander around the desks, rather than encountering obstacles or getting a feng shui speeding ticket?

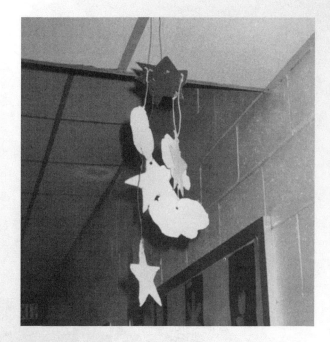

Chi stops to rest briefly at each mobile as it traverses this long hallway. Teachers in Springfield School placed these mobiles to prevent the chi from passing by their rooms.

Follow these suggestions:

- Resist the inclination to place desks in neat rows that face the center front of the classroom. Instead, arrange students in study groups, or in a semi-circular pattern.

- If straight rows are unavoidable, consider other ways to slow down the chi. Look at your floor tile patterns, for example. Is there a horizontal arrangement that would alternate light and dark? This slows chi as it stops to "look" at each change.

- Invite chi into the room by hanging a mobile by the door.

- Help the chi to move through your room with your students by placing free-flowing mobiles over their desks.

Just as important as the mobile by the door is something bright on the opposite wall. This draws the students and the chi into the room. Since most classrooms have windows opposite the door, hang another mobile. The sunlight will shimmer around your mobile, attracting your students into the room.

Chi Connects

Remember the connect-the-dots puzzles you liked as a child, the ones that your young students now enjoy? When the dots joined easily, the task was enjoyable and fulfilling as you saw the picture develop. If a number or two was omitted or missed, the task became frustrating.

Chi feels the same way. It needs to connect from one place in the room to another. It needs to find like items together. It needs to know that it will be able to bounce happily around the room, connecting all the animate and inanimate objects together as a unit.

How can you get your chi to connect, to make the room a unit rather than disjointed objects and people existing in one place?

Try these suggestions:

📌 GREAT IDEAS!

- Keep all similar objects in one place. It is easier to find a paper if all your file cabinets are in the same area. Keep all of your art-related materials on one side of the room. And store student supplies separate from teacher supplies.

- After reading the next chapter on the bagua, make sure you keep all the elements of an area together.

- Perhaps you are fortunate enough to have different colored chairs in your room. Alternate the chair colors in a regular pattern, rather than haphazardly around the room.

Chi Accumulates

This is an undesirable characteristic for chi. Because of the nature of chi to accumulate, it will easily transform from sheng chi to ssu chi if you are not careful. Just as water becomes still in a tidal pool until the next tide, chi will accumulate in areas of disuse. Since you want your chi to meander around your room, consider these suggestions for preventing chi from accumulating:

GREAT IDEAS!

- Eliminate clutter. For suggestions on how to accomplish this some-what-insurmountable task, see Chapter 6.

- Organize, organize, organize. Have a place for each item and label where it belongs. A number of years ago, I had a supervisor who required a room inventory. Although at the time I resented having to do yet another end-of-the-year task, it taught me to organize my classroom supplies so I could easily locate them.

- Learn to replace old items. As you get new supplies in September, discard an equal number of old, timeworn supplies.

Chi Changes

Chi goes through cycles like everything else. It is born, it grows, it weakens, and it dies. The object is to attract the sheng chi while dispelling the shar and ssu chi.

As a matter of fact, chi loves to see change. You know how satisfied you feel when you've just finished spring-cleaning or you moved around some of your furniture? It feels like a new beginning, right? That's because the chi (along with all the dust in that room) has been cleansed and shifted. The old, musty chi is gone and the fresh, spring-like chi has been born.

Now think about your classroom. When was the last time you gave your room a thorough cleaning? Certainly, the custodial staff cleans the floors and walls during the summer. I've seen the mess they make as they remove all of my furniture, polish the floors, wash the blackboards, and return the cabinets and desks to their original positions. But if your school is like mine, they leave the internal cleaning of the desks and cabinets to the teachers.

So, again, I ask—when was the last time you gave your room a thorough cleaning? Perhaps you can find out when your room is scheduled for its annual summer scrub. Go in before that time armed with dust rag and polish. Wipe down the shelves, dust off the books, and polish the woodwork. Then cover everything with newspaper so the dust doesn't return. After a day's work, when you return in September, your entire room will sparkle, not just the floors and the walls.

How else can you help your chi change?

GREAT IDEAS!

- Rotate bulletin boards frequently . . . not just the message, but the backing and border, as well.

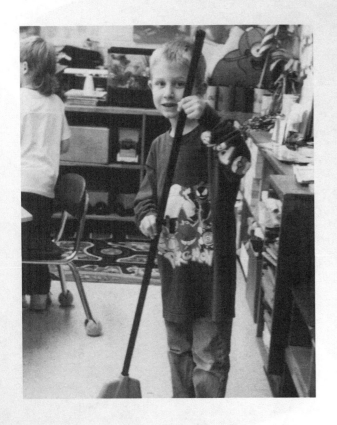

- Shift some of your games and books around. I can guarantee that your students will find things they never knew existed in your classroom.

- Change student seats. Keep the best-direction formula in mind when you do this so you maintain your students' comfort factors.

- Change one thing in your classroom each day. That may be as simple as tossing a dead flower, or as complex as setting up a helper schedule on the bulletin board.

- Schedule student desk clean-up days. This might be at the end of each week or the beginning of each month. Make sure you include *your* desk in the clean-up.

Learn to look at your classroom through the eyes of chi. When you walk into your classroom, do you feel comfortable moving among your students? Are you uplifted? Do you see daily change? If so, your chi is happy. And if your chi is happy, everyone and everything in the room will be comfortable.

◎ Yin and Yang

Yin and yang are natural opposites. Without one, the other would not exist. When in balance, yin and yang operate like a perpetual motion machine. If they become unbalanced, with one becoming stronger than the other, discord controls your life. You become ill, have problems with relationships, and may even have financial difficulties. When your world is balanced, you feel good, you produce well at work, and you generally are happy to be alive (Brown 1998).

Environmental unbalance wears away at your personal balance. If all the heavy furniture is on one side of the room, you will feel a physical imbalance. If there are deep, dark colors on one side of the room and pastel shades on the other, you will feel visual imbalance. Similarly, if there is too much noise on one side of the classroom and none on the other, you feel auditory imbalance. There are many ways in which your environment can become imbalanced.

Yin and yang operate in a cycle similar to chi. When the extreme of yang is reached, yin is born. When the extreme of yin is reached, yang is born. Let me give you an example from decorating history. During the Victorian Age, decorators used dark, heavy, velvet curtains. Accessories dripped with lace and flowers. Furniture crowded every square inch of wall space. In reaction to this extreme of decoration, the art nouveau style surfaced with its simplicity of style and form (Kicklighter and Kicklighter 1992).

In the classroom, yin and yang appear in different ways. Assign the boys to one side of the room and girls on the other and you produce instant imbalance. Placing all the passive students in the back and the active students in the front is also undesirable. These are two examples that modern teachers rarely use anymore.

YIN	YANG
Dark	Light
Night	Day
Cold	Hot
Soft	Hard
Earth	Sky
Neutral colors	Vibrant colors
Stillness	Movement
Low	High
Rounded	Angled
Quiet	Noisy
Dead	Alive
Passive	Active
Even	Odd
Valley	Hill
Winter	Summer
Sleep	Wakefulness
Fullness	Hunger
Simple	Elaborate
Plants	Rocks
Meek	Aggressive

However, there are many other ways that yin and yang interact in a classroom. Consider the chart of opposites listed on the left side of the page.

The classroom is an extremely yang environment. If you consider the bright lights, the youthful exuberance, and the colorful posters that attract young minds, you have a recipe for hyperactivity. In that first class where I discovered feng shui, my initial observations included the interaction of yin and yang. After I dimmed the lights and played calming music, my normally yang students drifted toward yin. All students are capable of alternating between yin and yang. It is your duty as their teacher to choose when and where each is activated. You want them yang on the playground, but yin during math lessons. You want them yang and full of energy when they start the day, but you want them yin during seatwork.

So how do we achieve this balance? Here are a number of suggestions:

GREAT IDEAS!

- Provide visual or auditory clues for the change from yin to yang. I turn off the lights when I want my students to listen, then put them back on when it is time for the students to work.

- Use your window shades. Too often, teachers ignore the extreme amount of bright light streaming in through the windows, adding to the already yang atmosphere. If it is especially sunny, pull the shades to eliminate some, but not all, of the sunlight coming into the room.

- Play appropriate background music during quiet times. Generally, if students are listening to the music, they will be less likely to generate their own conversations.

Several disorders, such as ADHD, Irlen Syndrome, and Sensory Integrative Dysfunction are aggravated by intense differences between light and dark. In several, unrelated studies, the extreme contrast (yin/yang) between the white paper and the black letters significantly decreased the participants' ability to read and comprehend.

Too much yang (white paper) is counterproductive when teaching children with certain disabilities. Irlen also found that too much fluorescent light is also detrimental to reading ability. Research supports feng shui. If the environment is balanced, students will learn easier.

In conclusion, the energy in a classroom is the result of the number of individuals plus the arrangement of furnishings in the room. When one works against the other, a negative arrangement occurs.

A greater sensitivity to environmental conditions can aid perceptual ease and comfort. (Irlen 1991, 186)

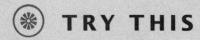

Create a room map (you will also need this for further activities). Measure the perimeter and location of windows and doors. Use a permanent marker to draw the outline of your room on graph paper where one square equals one foot. Then place this map in a clear page protector. Using an overhead marker on the plastic cover,

1. Identify the yin (-) and yang (+) areas. Are they all clustered to one side? In one corner? Or are they scattered evenly around the room, creating a balance of yin and yang? If they are clustered, suggest to yourself ways to redistribute the yin and yang elements for better balance.

2. Follow your chi through the room. Track your footsteps as you move through the room. Do you move effortlessly and fluidly? Or do you need to stop and turn before proceeding in a different direction? If the former is the case, rearrange your furniture so you can move more easily.

SAMPLE CLASSROOM MAP

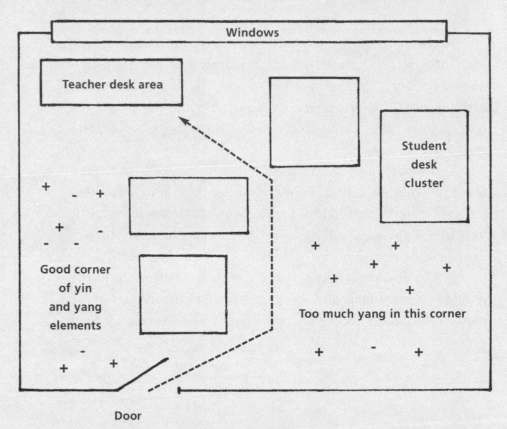

The teacher needs to make sharp turns in order to reach the desk area. The desk is also directly opposite the door and in front of a window, which allows shar chi to whip past the teacher.

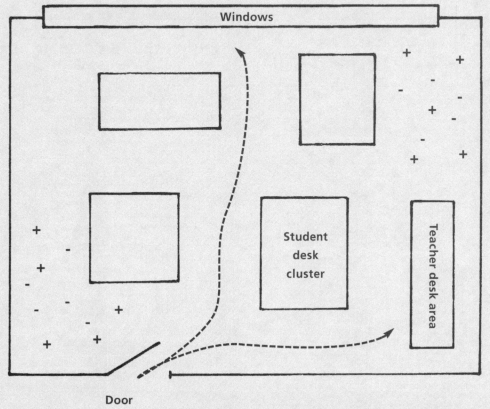

Windows

Student desk cluster

Teacher desk area

Door

The teacher's desk is in the command position—able to see the door, yet not directly in front of it.

Chi is better able to meander around the room without interruption.

A BETTER CLASSROOM ARRANGEMENT

4

A TEACHER'S BAGUA of TRICKS

Our lives tend to follow a natural progression. Generally, we are comfortable with that progression. We get up in the morning, do our daily routine (however complicated that may be if children are involved), go to work, come home, follow another routine at home (again, complicated by assorted carpools and sports practices), go to bed, and then start all over again the next day. Life follows cycles. Feng shui is no different. Each room follows a cycle, a rhythmic movement of chi.

A bagua illustrates the cycle of an environment. It is a powerful tool that, when used correctly, will make a significant difference in the classroom climate.

BAGUA: An eight-sided tool that provides the basis for analyzing the feng shui effectiveness of every area in a room.

Remember the game of "Careers" where you organized your love, fame, and money into neat columns on a score sheet? The bagua has the same effect in your classroom. It helps to organize all the desirable attributes of a classroom, such as education, relationships, and fame so that each has its own designated space. Specific numbers, elements, shapes, and colors influence each of those spaces. Your job, as you read this chapter, is to think about where you currently have the bagua characteristics in your room and, if they are out of place, where they should be relocated.

Bagua Basics

In ancient China, the bagua was an eight-sided figure that corresponded to eight directions of the compass. I prefer to use a nine-square quilt-style model because this makes the bagua easier to understand and reference for the generally square classrooms.

You will notice that the squared bagua appears to be upside down with north at the bottom of the compass. That is because the Chinese felt that the south, with its warming sun, was the preferable direction, so they placed it at the top, an honor location.

However, in Western feng shui, the compass directions are more of a guide to placement than they are a true compass orientation. In Western feng shui, the north, northeast, and northwest sectors indicate the three possible locations for the front door of the house or the entrance door of the classroom. Therefore, the far right corner of the classroom would be designated the southwest corner, whereas directly across from the door is considered south.

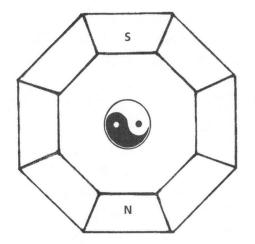

Southeast	South	Southwest
East	Center	West
Northeast	North	Northwest

◎ Bagua Numbers

Each section of a bagua is assigned a number. (See page 36.) As you might imagine, the arrangement of these numbers is not arbitrary. In fact, they are quite ordered and mathematical. When the numbers are connected, they not only form a perfectly balanced design, but each horizontal, vertical, and diagonal line adds up to fifteen. An even greater "coincidence" is that in ancient China, the number nine represented heaven, while six represented earth; another fifteen, and a perfect yin yang—heaven and earth. Another interesting coincidence is that there are nine planets in our solar system, yet the ancients were historically unaware of Uranus, Neptune, and Pluto (Skinner 2001).

My experience in working with the bagua map is that it is one of the most powerful ways to create positive changes and results in your life. Homes, office buildings, condominium complexes, gardens, rooms, and even furniture can be mapped out using this potent tool. I have seen it produce results that appear amazing and magical (Collins 1996, 61).

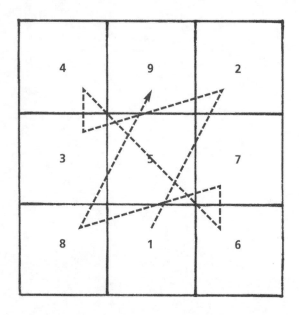

⊚ Bagua Elements

In addition to the numbers associated with each of the bagua sectors, different elements and their accompanying symbolism control each area. Feng shui recognizes five elements: wood, fire, water, earth, and metal.

Wood

Wood is the element of the east and southeast. It is the energy of birth and death; of growth and decay; of strength and flexibility. If you consider the characteristics of trees, you will understand the symbolism of wood. Wood in nature has roots for support. A tree begins small, but eventually grows to enormous heights, branching and developing into a magnificent specimen. However, as with all in nature, trees die, but in that death, they support life. It is an amazing cycle, and especially symbolic for educators.

Wood in your classroom takes the form of the furniture and plants. It also takes the form of wood-based textiles such as cotton and, less frequently, linen. So, desks, cabinets, tables, books, cotton cloths, cotton rope, floral prints, and plants represent the wood element.

The shape associated with wood is the rectangle, both vertical, as trees grow upward, and horizontal, at the end of their cycle when they fall and nourish new life. This shape is found in columns, stripes, tall filing cabinets, and books.

Green, rather than brown, represents the wood element because it is important to focus on the growth cycle, rather than the decay cycle, of this element. New growth in the spring is a bright green. Summer growth, with its nourishing chlorophyll, is a deep green.

Fire

Fire is the element of the south. It is the energy of the sun, light, and warmth. Sunlight brings life to all it touches. It stimulates the use of chlorophyll in plants and Vitamin D in humans. Fire is also destructive, but again in that destruction, comes new life. Consider the pygmy pine forests where regular fires are necessary to the survival of the woodlands. It seems as if nature is saying that change is good when improvement is a result of that change.

Fire in your classroom takes the form of the sunlight streaming through your windows and animals, including humans. It also takes the form of materials made from animals, such as silk, fur, and leather. Although feng shui generally does not recognize synthetic materials, the human animal creates them, so materials such as plastic are considered part of the fire element. Therefore, a hamster in a cage, a science center displaying a shed snakeskin, blue jay feathers, whale teeth, a Native American wool blanket, or a picture of Abraham Lincoln all represent fire. Likewise, your Styrofoam food pyramid and plastic storage boxes symbolize fire.

The shape associated with fire is the triangle in all its forms. This can be a three-dimensional pyramid, a star placed on excellent work, or an inverted ice cream cone. Fire symbols attract attention because they are pointed.

Red in all its tints and shades is naturally the fire color. Red is an energizing color, but when used too often it becomes overwhelming. Just as a small fire in the fireplace is comforting, a fire in the house is destructive. Be careful not to use too much red in your classroom.

All children appreciate some form of positive recognition.

When a water feature accompanies a lesson, another dimension of interest is added.

Water

Water is the element of the north. It is the energy of fluid movement and cleansing. It is reflective and adaptive, fitting into the shape of its container. Of course, water can also be destructive when allowed to overflow its container, whether that container is the bathtub or a riverbed. The message sent by the water element is flexibility and moderation.

Water in your classroom takes the form of all water features, reflective surfaces, and free-form shapes. Therefore, the fish tank, sink, mirror, windows, ocean pictures, and scalloped bulletin board borders represent the water feature. This is probably the least represented element in our classrooms, especially in the upper grades where the only water elements might be the windows, and perhaps a scalloped border.

Naturally, blue and black are the colors of the water element. Both rich royal blue and calming midnight blue can be successfully used in these areas. Black should be used sparingly.

Earth

Earth is the element of the southeast, northwest, and center. It is the energy of soil that nourishes and supports life. Just as with the other elements, it can also be destructive, especially when combined with the water element to produce mudslides. The earth element reminds us to nurture what is important to us before it is gone.

Earth in your classroom takes the form of stones, ceramics, bricks, and tiles. Clay flowerpots, brick walls, and ceramic sculptures represent the earth element. Posters depicting amber waves of grain or sand dunes represent the earth element, also.

As you might expect, the earth colors are the warm ambers rusts and ochre. They are also the colors of turquoise, diamond, and quartz. Beautiful crystals with facets reflecting sunlight belong to the earth element.

The earth shape, however, is square, not round. The logic here is that according to the ancient Chinese, the earth was flat and the garden plots were divided into squares of crops.

Metal

Metal is the element of the northwest and west. It is the energy of ores found deep within the earth. These ores are at the same time valuable and dangerous—valuable when used as currency or cures, but dangerous when used to create weapons. The metal element carries a warning to be careful with our possessions lest they be used for destructive rather than productive purposes.

Metal in your classroom takes the form of all metal objects. Look up and you may see metal I-beams traversing your classroom, or metal pipes and wires in conduits. Aluminum frames on bulletin boards and posters belong to the metal element.

Metal's colors are white, gray, and all metallics: gold, copper, and silver. Metal's shape is round, reminiscent of the round beads of water that condense on cold metal surfaces. Circles, ovals, and arches represent metal throughout your room.

A homemade metallic mobile might include old CDs and bits of metal jewelry.

A key principle of feng shui is the way the Five Elements react and influence each other. Many of a feng shui consultant's suggestions for solutions to current business problems are based on an analysis of how the different elements, and the chi energy associated with them, combine in a building (Brown 1998, 17).

Combinations

Combinations of elements are also important to the feng shui of classrooms. Just as a sausage pizza contains all of the food groups, some objects around you contain parts of all the elements. Take, for example, a fish or reptile tank. It has the water element, but there is also fire in the animals, earth in the sand, metal in the frame, and wood in the plants. Concentrating elements into one object is an excellent way to ensure that all the elements are represented in an area. Although each sector should consist primarily of its key element, each sector should also include some of all the elements to prevent the primary element from becoming too overwhelming and dominant.

You do not need to have a unified object like a fish tank in order to have a combination of elements. You may, on a display table for Metric Day (October 10), have ten pennies (metal), ten tiles (earth), a plant with ten branches (wood), a mirror reflecting the plant with ten branches (water), and ten feathers (fire). The possibilities are endless.

☺ Bagua Significance

In addition to having elements, numbers, and shapes in each section, the bagua demands certain significance to each area. This is the most interesting area of feng shui because it shows how to energize areas of your classroom that need improvement. Consider the chart on the following page.

Each area of the room represents a different focus of classroom significance. Perhaps you have travel posters all around the room. This may be acceptable if you are a foreign language teacher, but in the elementary classroom, these travel posters should be concentrated in the northwest corner of your classroom.

But suppose you are a foreign language teacher. Is it acceptable to place your travel posters wherever there is space? Absolutely not. Consider the color and content of your posters. Those with pictures of mountains belong in the south or west, depending on whether they are pointed (south) or rolling hills (west). Posters that depict two people together should be in the southwest, while pictures of forests go in the east or southeast.

Look at this chart with suggestions for each corner and add your own ideas from your own classroom.

SE Possessions, wealth	S Recognition, fame	SW Friendship, partners
E Family, health	Self	W Creativity, children
NE Knowledge, discovery	N Careers, success	NW Diversity, travel

BAGUA SECTION	SUGGESTION	YOUR IDEAS
SE — Possessions	Student project storage	
S — Recognition	Student achievement banner	
SW — Friendship	Conflict resolution table	
E — Family	Classroom photographs	
W — Creativity	Art supplies, think-abouts	
NE — Knowledge	Books, globe	
N — Careers	Career posters or costumes	
NW — Diversity	Multicultural exhibit	

You should now see that each area of the bagua carries with it a special significance. It is an organizational device to help you strategically place the puzzle pieces of your classroom so they all come together in an orderly fashion. This is why feng shui is so effective. People, especially children, react more positively in an organized environment.

If you want to energize a particular area of the room, simply arrange your furniture and other classroom elements according to the numbers, shapes, and elements prescribed by the bagua. Maybe some students do not appreciate the diverse cultures brought by other students into the room. Energize your diversity corner—perhaps you could hang a metal wind chime with six chimes near a "children of the world" poster. Each time you hear a disparaging remark against a child, ring the chimes to draw your students' attention to the fact that together they create the world as it exists in your classroom.

One more example. If you have a weekly or monthly theme, use the northeast corner to display objects related to that theme. Suppose you are celebrating Women's History Month. On a square table, perhaps covered with a turquoise cloth, you might include eight items related to women's history. Remember to include something from each of Gardner's "intelligences":

1. A Susan B. Anthony coin
2. Sheet music (Pearl Bailey)
3. A flag (Betsy Ross)
4. Ice skates (Kristi Yamaguchi)
5. A copy of *Jane Eyre* (Charlotte Brontë)

6. A bus ticket (Rosa Parks)

7. Reproduction of Nobel peace prize (Marie Curie)

8. A stuffed monkey (Jane Goodall)

By now your mind is probably traveling around the room, seeing things in a new perspective, mentally moving them to where they belong. Use the following chart to further organize your room and your ideas.

Reproduce the following bagua on an overhead sheet, then place it over your room plan. What do you find in each section? Do you have a tall wooden file cabinet in the metal section, which cries out for circles and ovals? Do you have a picture of five people in the relationships corner, which should have an even number of pairs? For now, just indicate the areas that need improvement. In the next chapter you will learn how to fix these problems.

▬	▲	■
SE — Possessions 4 Wood Green, purple	S — Recognition 9 Fire Red	SW — Friendship 2 Earth Yellow
▬	■	●
E — Family 3 Wood Green	Self 5 Earth Orange	W — Creativity 7 Metal White
■	〜	●
NE — Knowledge 8 Earth Turquoise	N — Careers 1 Water Blue, black	NW — Diversity 6 Metal Gray, white

REMEDIES for the NOT-SO-PERFECT CLASSROOM

So now you know where things are supposed to go, but it may not happen for any number of reasons:

1. The superintendent refuses to approve the relocation of the water pipes that go directly through your "fire" area.

2. The janitors don't have time to take down the built-in wooden cabinets that are creating negative energy in your "earth" corner.

3. The janitors don't have time to rebuild those cabinets in the "wood" area.

4. There just isn't any other place in the room that will accommodate your computers because the electricians put the power strip in your "wood" area.

Don't despair. Help is on the way. In fact, much of feng shui is all about remedies. Few people are fortunate enough to start out in a new school with new equipment ready to implement feng shui suggestions on the first day of classes. Most teachers do the best they can in an aging structure with antiquated furniture and teaching aids left over from 1978. But even your best effort can be improved with feng shui remedies.

◎ Bagua Cycles

Life follows cycles. And so do the feng shui elements, which are arranged in three cycles:

- **Supporting**—one element helps another element
- **Destroying**—one element drains the effects of another element
- **Regulating**—one element controls another element

If you consider the characteristics of the elements again, you will see how these cycles work in an environment. Consider the areas in your room where you need to improve the Feng Shui treatments as you read this chapter.

The Supporting Cycle

- Wood fuels fire
- Fire creates ash, forming earth
- Earth develops metal
- Metal forms water droplets on the surface
- Water nourishes wood
- And the cycle starts all over again

You would use the Supporting Cycle if you want to stimulate an element. This might be necessary if you want to energize a section of the room or help one element overcome another element. Consider this scenario. You have a peace table set up in the southwest corner, but you don't think stones associated with the earth element would be an appropriate addition for obvious reasons. Also, the wood of the table feeds on the earth, draining that element from your peace corner. Therefore, you would use the fire element to support earth. Put a happy-face–printed tablecloth on the table. Add a small lamp to focus your students' attention to the task at hand. When you use the supporting element in an earth area, you may not need the designated element in order to energize that area.

In the Supporting Cycle, wood fuels fire.

The Destroying Cycle

The Destroying Cycle
- Water extinguishes fire
- Fire melts metal
- Metal cuts wood
- Wood pulls from the earth
- Earth dams water
- And the cycle starts all over again

The Inert Relationships
- Earth, as solid rock, will not support wood
- Wood has no impact on metal
- Metal cannot fuel a fire
- Fire cannot exist in water
- Water filters through the earth

You would use the Destroying Cycle if you have an immovable object in a section of the room where the element it represents would destroy the significance of the area, thereby reducing the effectiveness of the feng shui in your room. Consider this scenario to illustrate the Destroying Cycle. The only place you can locate your computers is on the east wall, the worst feng shui location for any electronics or metal equipment. This is your family area where you should be displaying everything about your classroom family. The main element for this wall is wood. Metal, in the form of electronics, cuts wood. Therefore, you need fire to melt the metal. How do you do that? In the same way you used the fire element to support earth in your friendship corner. You don't need to use the same happy-face fabric, although you could do that for unification. Instead, consider placing a poster of a volcano on that wall, or arrange classroom photographs in a mountain pattern.

The Reducing Cycle

- Earth controls fire
- Fire consumes wood
- Wood soaks water
- Water corrodes metal
- Metal contains earth
- And the cycle starts all over again

Finally, you would use the Reducing Cycle when there are overwhelming primary and supporting elements in an area of your room. Therefore, the elements don't need to be destroyed, merely reduced. Consider this scenario to illustrate the Reducing Cycle. Your whiteboard is located on the west "creativity" wall. A metal strip frames the whiteboard. Your walls are painted a light yellow. Everything in this area screams "metal" because the yellow (earth) walls support the aluminum framed whiteboard (metal). Turn down the visual volume by adding a water feature like a wavy blue border directly on the whiteboard. This will have the added benefit of helping your children focus on your notes. Remember that your ultimate goal is balance. You can have too much of a good feng shui thing!

Remember, too, that you should have a blend of feng shui elements in each area. Consider the "possessions" and "cooperation" areas, which have wood as the controlling element. Wood should certainly dominate that area. However, it should not be the only element there. Introduce some water to support the wood. Highlight with a bit of fire to stop the wood from

In the Reducing Cycle, earth controls fire.

commanding that area. Then, add just a touch of the destructive metal and earth elements. Confused yet? This chart should help:

USE MOSTLY THE DOMINANT ELEMENT	THEN ADD SOME OF THE SUPPORTING ELEMENT	HIGHLIGHT WITH THE REDUCING ELEMENT	ADD JUST A BIT OF THE DESTROYING ELEMENTS:
Wood	Water	Fire	Metal and Earth
Fire	Wood	Earth	Water and Metal
Earth	Fire	Metal	Wood and Water
Metal	Earth	Water	Fire and Wood
Water	Metal	Wood	Earth and Fire

◉ Poison Arrows

Did you ever notice that the corners of Chinese pagodas are always turned upwards? That is because in feng shui, pointed objects are as detrimental to health and wellness as actual weapons. The Chinese turn the corners of the pagodas upward so as to deflect the poison arrows from people who pass by.

Which of these poison arrows or sheng chi influences do you have in your classroom?

_____ Long, overhead beams

_____ Desks in rows

_____ Objects that point downward from the ceiling

_____ Classroom door at the end of a long hallway

_____ Sharp corners on tables and cabinets

_____ Square pillars

If you do, you may use some of the following remedies.

📌 GREAT IDEAS!

- Add a mirror to reflect the sharp corners of pillars or cabinets back to the object, thereby containing the poison arrows within.

- Rearrange your desks so that they are not in a straight line.

- Hang garlands from the overhead beams.

- Wrap seasonal fabric strips around pillars.

- If your classroom is at the end of a long hallway, hang a mirror outside of your classroom to reflect the sheng chi.

CAUTION! Be very careful where you place corrective measures that deflect poison arrows. The energy you repel from one area may harm another.

Remember that bruise you got when you bumped into the edge of a table? Not only is the chi harmful, but it is also poor

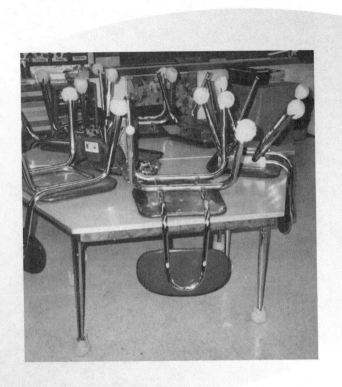

decorating sense to locate a table where you could easily bump into it. If you are unable to move the table or cabinets, then use rubber bumpers available from most hardware stores to soften the edges. I have even seen some teachers use old tennis balls that have been sliced open, then glued to the corners.

Missing Corners

In addition to considering the elements and their impact on a room, it is important to look at the room as a whole. Feng shui recognizes that not all rooms are square, although certainly most classrooms are square or rectangular. Even if you have a closet in one corner of your room that gives the illusion that the room is not perfectly square, the overall dimensions of the room probably create a square shape. However, yours may take on different shapes.

In Room A, the northwest "diversity" corner is missing. A teacher in this classroom may notice extremely prejudicial remarks and actions. There might be a lack of appreciation for different cultures. With the "diversity" corner missing, children may lose direction when multicultural topics are discussed.

In Room B, the north "careers" area is missing. A teacher in this classroom could notice that his or her students have a lack of direction or motivation because they don't see any reason to study or become involved in classwork.

In feng shui, there are four basic remedies that work in a classroom: light, sound, motion, and reflection. How do these

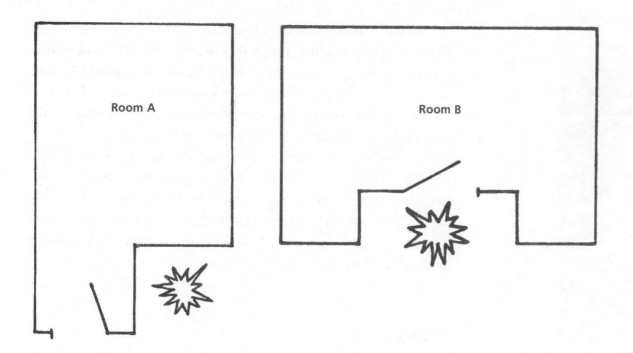

remedies help fix the missing areas? They confuse the chi into thinking that the area is actually there. Consider that the missing area is yin—it is dark, quiet, and still. It needs a balance of yang to come alive. Each of the remedies introduces a yang feature near the missing area. Consider each remedy individually.

Light

Light lifts chi and energizes any area it visits. Chi thinks a missing area is dark, and therefore not worthy of its attention. By

When children play outside, the chi of sunlight energizes them. They carry this positive chi back into the classroom.

focusing a light in that area to brighten it, you can tell the chi that the area is not missing, but merely hiding behind a solid wall. I know that sounds crazy, but the energy in chi is powerful and needs to circulate whether through a real or an imagined area.

So what can you use as light in a missing area? You certainly wouldn't use a candle with an open flame in a classroom, but light in the form of a refracting crystal is wonderful. Floor lamps or table lamps can be used to brighten a missing sector. You may even brighten a dark corner with a plant adorned with mini-lights. If you are fortunate enough to have a window in that missing corner, then no further remedy is needed. The natural sunlight will attract chi to that area.

Music

Music attracts everyone, but especially youth. The most primitive musical instruments were drums and flutes. The sounds they produced sent messages to people near and far. The energy of these instruments was powerful in that they became a form of communication between tribes. Sounds can be used in a classroom to stimulate the chi in missing areas. No, you're not going to install a set of drums in your room. But you can place a wind chime near the missing corner. Wind chimes combine the percussion of drums and resonance of the flute into one instrument.

Choose your wind chimes carefully, as there are many on the market. Look to see what area is missing. If it is the "diversity" corner, then choose a chime with six metal tubes suspended in a circular pattern. Be careful that the clapper is neither wood nor fire (triangle or animal shape). Instead, find one with a ceramic clapper. Or perhaps your "possessions" corner is missing. There, you should hang a wind chime that has four bamboo flutes and a wood or purple-colored clapper. Get the idea? Choose your wind chime according to the bagua for maximum effectiveness.

Another way to use sound to energize the missing corner is to place a CD player there, provided this is not your "possessions" or "family" areas, where the electronic, metal parts of the CD player will cut the controlling wood element. Play appropriate music for your different activities throughout the day. For example, during silent reading time, play Mozart. During clean-up, play Sousa. Chris Brewer (1995) feels that the emotional rhythms created by music in the classroom aids student concentration. Playing background music helps them to focus their thoughts on the task at hand.

Balance your music with silence. Remember—feng shui is all about balance. Yin silence should be balanced with yang music, even if you don't have a missing corner.

Motion

Motion attracts chi's attention. Imagine that you're reading with one group of students and out of the corner of your eye you see another student, who is supposed to be working at his or her seat, heading for the art supplies. Or perhaps it is Saturday, and you pass by a new gas station. The owner has strung a truckload of triangular flags around his property, which flap in the wind. In both cases, the motion attracts your attention.

So how can you use motion to disguise missing corners in a classroom? You might want to hang a spiraling, rainbow-colored mobile near the missing corner. Or you might simply move a clock to that area. Any motion, however small, will energize a missing area by circulating the chi around it.

Mirrors

Mirrors reflect the missing corner back into the room. Interior designers have used this method for many years to make a small area appear larger. That is exactly what you want to do—make the nonexistent corner appear by using a mirror to reflect the rest of the room into that area. Mirrors, as symbols of both water and metal elements, are particularly effective in the "careers" and "diversity" areas for masking missing corners.

Aromatherapy

Aromatherapy is powerful. Funky classroom odors require their own special remedies. From adolescent gym class odors to unique chemical odors in a lab, classroom odors present particularly pungent problems. I use orange peels to mask both purchased and natural student scents. If you don't have a ceramic dish, place the peels in a plastic berry box for ventilation, either on your desk or just inside the door. When the peels dry, their effectiveness wanes. The students understand my motivation, so after lunch periods I am usually presented with more orange peels than I can

If you have access to a ceramics studio, you can make your own aromatherapy pot by cutting holes in the side of greenware before it is fired, as the student above has done for me. If left unglazed, the ceramic will absorb the orange oils.

use in a month. Not only do I get a natural air freshener for my room, but the students have also begun eating more oranges. When I first started this practice, a former student walked in and remarked, "Your room has a welcoming odor." I knew I had achieved my goal.

Feng shui remedies can be used to repair all areas of your classroom. Whether you have immovable objects in the wrong area of the room or you have a missing area that you want to replace, the remedies will help make your room feng shui compliant.

Everything in your environment may have some impact on your health. (NIEHS Kids Pages)

TRY THIS

To see the effect of feng shui balance on an unbalanced area, follow these steps:

1. Choose an area that needs a remedy—a missing corner, a poison arrow, a wrong element, etc.

2. Determine the controlling element.

3. Follow the "Remedies Chart" and add the wrong element to that area.

4. Leave your test area in that condition for a week.

5. Record students' grades, behavior, and attitude while they are in that area.

6. The next week, follow the "Remedies Chart" by eliminating the destructive element and adding the supporting element.

7. Again, record students' grades, behavior, and attitude while they are in that area.

8. Notice the difference.

6

ARE YOU a CLUTTER BUG?

Before you can begin to implement feng shui arrangements and remedies, you need a clutter-free environment. What is clutter? It is a collection of things in your environment that you no longer use or love. Clutter is a permanent messiness and should not be confused with the temporary messiness associated with complex art projects or the fervor of a busy day.

Clutter is like stagnant water, a collection of ssu chi waiting to snag you and suck you into a dingy place unworthy of anything beautiful. Look around your classroom—is the chi gently moving around, meandering among organized cabinets, dusted

Which desk looks more like yours?

bookcases, and uncluttered desks, including your own? Or is it trapped in corners, snagged by piles of unfiled papers, and churning aimlessly around items more suited for the dumpster? Does your room bear more resemblance to a junkyard than a classroom?

◎ What Is Your Room Style?

1. *The stored items in your room are . . .*
   A. always labeled and in a designated space.
   B. generally organized by use.
   C. disorganized, but you usually find what you need.
   D. so jumbled that it takes you ten minutes to find your role book.

2. *When you first walk into your room, you . . .*
   A. feel welcomed by the arrangement.
   B. feel the need to make a list of places that need attention.
   C. are overwhelmed by the clutter, but have learned to live with it.
   D. want to walk back out, discouraged by the total lack of order.

3. *Most of your students . . .*
   A. neatly organize their desks.
   B. have stray papers peeking from the edge of the desk.
   C. lose their belongings frequently.
   D. are so disorganized that they take several minutes to find a notebook.

4. *The top of your desk . . .*

   A. has only the necessary items and is always clean.

   B. has necessary items, but is dusty.

   C. has a mixture of necessary items, ungraded papers, assignments from last week, and a small Lost and Found Department.

   D. should be declared a national disaster area.

5. *Your file cabinet . . .*

   A. contains only two copies of each ditto arranged in alphabetical or chronological order.

   B. contains many copies of current dittos and material "you may use some day."

   C. contains dittos from other teachers who used your room in 1986.

   D. is so packed that you need a pry bar to move the folders.

6. *Your bulletin boards . . .*

   A. contain current material, neatly arranged on a bright background.

   B. offer some new and old information on faded construction paper.

   C. have been up since September with no change.

   D. are so cluttered, they serve no useful purpose for you or the students.

7. *Your window area . . .*

   A. has healthy plants and a neat display of student achievements.

   B. has a collection of unrelated items in daily use.

   C. is cluttered with many items that have outlived their usefulness.

   D. should be declared another national disaster area.

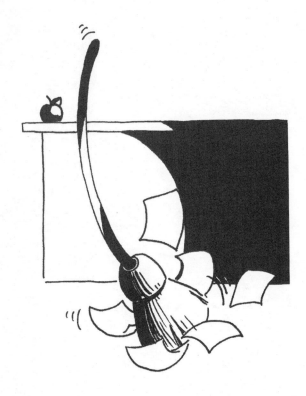

Now total your answers. As are 4 points, Bs are 3, Cs are 2, and Ds are 1. How did you score?

28–24 POINTS: **Mighty Tidy**
19–23 POINTS: **Stress Mess**
12–17 POINTS: **Jumble Gym**
7–11 POINTS: **Grime Scene**

Obviously, you can see that all of the "A" answers relate to a completely clutter-free environment, while the "D" answers are indicative of classrooms that should have a dumpster located outside of the window or door for easy access. Most of you probably have a mixture of "B" and "C" answers. This means that you are a normal, active teacher who finds that time spent planning and implementation of lessons is more productive than cleaning out old files. However, the benefit derived from decluttering your classroom will positively impact the effectiveness of those lessons you so carefully plan.

You're probably curious why Question 3 refers to your students rather than to you. That is because a clutter-free environment is contagious. If you are neat and organized, most students will likely pick up your habits.

So, if your classroom is "Mighty Tidy," congratulations on maintaining the optimal learning environment, free from clutter and distraction. If you have a "Stress Mess," reserve some time to relieve the everyday stress of teaching and begin decluttering. If you teach in a "Jumble Gym," start decluttering in small doses so you don't become overwhelmed by a seemingly endless task. And if your room is a "Grime Scene," order the dumpster as soon as possible.

⦿ There Is No Excuse for Clutter

Arlean Lambert, a librarian at Marshall School in South Orange, New Jersey, told me this story she uses to illustrate the effect of one effort toward decluttering an area.

There once was a woman who had such a messy, cluttered, house that she decided to leave. She felt weighed down and depressed by the mountain of work that needed to be done. While out of her house, she picked a single beautiful flower.

"This flower," she said to herself, "will surely brighten my house."

She returned with her flower and placed it in a vase. But the vase was dirty and dingy, so she washed it until it sparkled and was worthy of her beautiful flower.

She set it on her kitchen counter, but the counter was covered with dirty dishes and grime. So she washed the dishes and scrubbed the counter until it shined. Then she set the lovely flower in its sparkling vase on the shiny counter.

"My home is now clean," she said as she tried to find a place to sit and admire the clean area of her kitchen. But every seat was covered with old magazines and dirty clothes. So she . . .

Well, you get the message. One thing led to another and eventually, her whole house was worthy of that single beautiful flower. Is your classroom worthy of a single beautiful flower? Or is it like that woman's house?

Could you tolerate one beautiful flower in a messy kitchen?

Before

◎ Create a Plan to Declutter

The first step toward decluttering your classroom is to envision your room as it could be. You might draw a picture or floor plan of how you'd like to see your room. Or cut pictures from old school supply catalogs that show well-organized classrooms. If possible, visit classrooms of teachers who organize effectively. This is all part of the envisionment process. It jump-starts your brain. You don't need to copy the other teacher's classroom, nor do you need to pester your principal for new storage cabinets. You just need to start thinking about decluttering and reorganization.

After you envision your ultimate goal, you can begin to declutter, because without models and motivation, it's difficult to begin decluttering. Certainly it is possible, but like a diet, you will likely go back to your old ways without the models and motivation.

Close your eyes. Imagine a clean, uncluttered classroom. Perhaps one that is in a new school and you are the first teacher in that room. What will you include? Where will you put it? Why will you put it there? These are all the questions you should ask yourself when looking at the individual items in your classroom now.

Try placing decluttering mantras in places you look frequently—the front of your roll book, on your desk, or over the blackboard. Try these, or make up some of your own:

- Clutter Kills Creativity
- Neat Is Sweet
- Don't Disguise, Organize

As you look around your room, you probably feel overwhelmed and wonder where to begin. Start with a small area. If you wonder where to begin, start with your desk. The whole key to successful decluttering is to bite off small pieces at a time. It's also a good idea to keep a decluttering journal so you can track your progress.

◉ Decluttering Can Be Fun

Designate a time when you are neither tired nor hungry, put on some happy music, and get to work. Some successful declutterers come to school early to sift through old files or to label boxes (that have first been cleaned and sorted). This starts the day with a positive attitude. Even if you have only ten minutes each day, by the end of the week, you will have put in nearly an hour of decluttering activity.

Enlist the aid of a clutter buddy. Like the concept of a diet buddy, you can encourage each other, share each other's successes, and help each other overcome obstacles to successfully meet your goal.

Mike Nelson (2002) takes a no-nonsense approach to the relationship between feng shui and clutter. He feels that if a pile of clutter stops you from getting to or even seeing a particular part of your classroom, it doesn't take a feng shui master to understand that the pile should be eliminated.

Enlist your students as "Clutter Busters." Help them to identify areas that need to be organized or cleaned. As they look

After

around the room at their lower height, they will see areas in need of attention that you may have overlooked. Create a clutter suggestion box where students might add their own ideas for improvement, such as "Keep all backpacks off the floor," or "Have a desk clean-up time every Friday." Provide "Clutter Buster" awards for the student who has the neatest desk, finds the most clutter, or cleans the most shelves.

Place trash cans in strategic locations, not just by your desk or the door. One eighth-grade teacher I know placed his recycle bin directly under the paper cutter so the ragged edges of torn notebook paper could drop directly into the container. A fourth-grade teacher used natural orange-scented cleaner to wipe down the desktops. Not only does this product not need to be rinsed, it left a refreshing fragrance in the room. Consider other ways that your room can easily become cleaner and less cluttered.

◉ Where Is Your Clutter?

There is both obvious and disguised clutter in a classroom. Obvious clutter is what you try to put away before Parents' Night. Disguised clutter is the file cabinet filled with old dittos, desk drawers that hold confiscated items from five years ago, and storage cabinets that have never been organized. Both forms of clutter affect the movement of chi.

Tackle the obvious clutter first. Ever wonder why corners become clutter traps? It's because we naturally try to soften edges and round corners, filling in the area made by a right angle. Chi also likes soft edges and round corners. Chi emanates from the center of a room in a circular pattern, much like the ripples in water when you drop a pebble into the lake. What happens when this swirling chi finds a square corner? It becomes psychically sticky, trapped with no way out. As more chi becomes trapped in the corners, less is available to energize your classroom.

How can you soften those corners? You can try a number of suggestions.

📌 GREAT IDEAS!

- Hang a drape from one side of the corner to the other (remember to use the appropriate color and pattern for that corner as it applies to the controlling element). Behind that drape, neatly stack your labeled boxes, preferably on shelves so the custodial staff can easily clean the floor.

- Use a Japanese screen style of barrier. This is very effective in a reading corner where you can use the screen to post pictures related to the text.

- Place wood or metal shelves (again, consider the controlling element for the corner) diagonally. If you are concerned about the visible cavity formed behind the shelves, string holiday lights behind them.

- Hang knotted rope or a bead curtain from the ceiling across the corner. Attach clothespins at regular intervals and hang student work. This is especially good in the recognition or possessions area of your room.

Clutter likes to hide in boxes, closets, drawers, and even on your computer hard drive. The boxes are easy. Taking one box at a time and one item at a time, ask yourself these questions:

- Do I really need this?
- Is this outdated?
- Does this belong elsewhere with similar items?
- Is this a duplicate of something else?
- Can I share this with someone?
- Do I love this item?

You might think that last question is a bit absurd, but when you look at a box of broken crayons that have melted because the box was left on the window ledge last spring, you won't be able to cling to it as easily.

Each item you remove from a box should head toward one of six locations:

- Trash can
- Recycle bin
- Back in the box
- Elsewhere in the room
- Home
- Shared with others

Consider your files. You only need two copies of each ditto that you re-use each year, one to keep for your files and one to use at the copy machine. Recycle the rest. The next time you reach for that ditto, you will be more likely to edit the content for the current year if you don't feel obligated to begin with using up the fifteen copies that were left over from last year. If you keep those original two copies in a plastic sleeve inside a ring binder, your files will improve dramatically in only a few clean-up sessions.

Your computer files can be just as cluttered as your metal file cabinet. Set aside time to sort through those files you no longer use—or love—and delete or save to a separate disk. Then defrag your computer and the virtual chi will find it easier to travel around looking for a file.

◉ More Reasons to Declutter a Room

Aside from the feng shui benefits of decluttering, removing old and unused items from your room reduces safety hazards and infestation potential. If yours is a science classroom, old chemicals break down over time, changing their characteristics and, therefore, their usefulness. Cardboard boxes clustered in corners and closets invite vermin to take up residence in your room. Neither situation is desirable. So, if for no other reason, remove the clutter from your classroom to enjoy a safe environment.

Consider the observations by Robert M. Corrigan (2001):

- Pests gravitate toward cluttered areas because clutter enables pests to hide and reproduce, undisturbed from predators and people.
- Some cockroaches, ants, and silverfish prefer the various types of crevices layered clutter (e.g., stacks of paper) provide.

Chi needs to move inside your computer as easily as it moves around your decluttered room.

- Clutter can be dangerous. The brown recluse spider (*Loxosceles reclusa*) prefers to hide among layered papers and within forgotten boxes of cluttered corners, and similar areas. The poisonous brown recluse spiders and other pests have bitten children and teachers reaching into clutter piles to retrieve papers or other items.
- Rodents take advantage of clutter. It is not uncommon for two or three families of mice (15–20 mice) to share the base of one cardboard box in a classroom's cluttered closet.
- Pest control efforts are impossible in cluttered areas.
- Custodial cleaning efforts are diluted or impossible in cluttered classrooms.

Be careful of clutter around vents. Leave plenty of space for the air to circulate into and out of the room. A study by the Massachusetts Department of Public Health revealed that classrooms with closed or blocked air vents had carbon dioxide levels higher than 800 parts per million (ppm). An acceptable level of carbon dioxide is 600–800 ppm, while less than 600 ppm is preferable. Several classrooms that had blocked intake and exhaust vents were studied, and had a carbon dioxide level of over 1,100 ppm.

◉ Declutter Yourself, Too

While you are decluttering, remember that it is important to drink plenty of water to cleanse yourself as you cleanse your room. The flat, lifeless water we get from the spigot or bottles

---

Many students with visual impairments are distracted by loud noises, the hum of fluorescent lights, a visually cluttered classroom, and verbal commotion by others in the same environment. Students with visual impairments require organization and structure to maintain control over their learning environments (Sacks and Silberman 1999, Web site).

can be enhanced into an energizing beverage by pouring it back and forth between glasses to aerate it before drinking. If you are asthmatic or have other respiratory problems, consider wearing a mask while you declutter. Play relaxing, yet motivating music.

Only declutter when you are feeling well. Forget every other problem you have while you declutter. Open the windows and doors for ventilation while you work. If it is cold outside, open the window enough to bring in circulation. Take a deep, cleansing breath of fresh air, then start cleaning and organizing. When you are done, wash your hands to cleanse yourself before going on to other activities.

Decluttering is about letting go. It is about assigning priorities to objects in your room. It is about ener-chi efficiency. It is about defining funk-tion. (If the object is funky because of age, odor, or usefulness, then it needs to find a new home, perhaps in the dumpster.) Even those old projects you've saved over the years as examples should be discarded. If you are sentimentally attached to them, photograph them and create an album of great projects your students have created over the years.

The positive effects of decluttering are overwhelming. Almost instantly you feel an energy that proclaims your classroom a welcoming environment. The students will also feel this ener-chi that invigorates them to better performance.

If you share a room with a teacher who does not feel as strongly as you do about decluttering, don't despair. As you rearrange, neaten, and clean your part of the room, whether it is a cart or a designated cabinet and desk, your new attitude toward clutter will influence your colleague.

Even if your "classroom" is mobile, it can be arranged according to the bagua.

Continue to maintain your clutter-free classroom. Spend a few minutes at the beginning or end of each week cleaning and decluttering so the chi can maintain a happy trail around your room. As new supplies arrive in September, toss the same number of old, used, taking-up-room-in-the-closet supplies to make room for the shiny, new, filled-with-potential supplies. Remember to defrag your computer occasionally. The benefits you reap from a few minutes of cleaning and decluttering will repay you many times over in time saved looking for lost files and supplies.

Decluttering your classroom is not a practice; it is a way of life.

CHECK OUT THESE WEB SITES TO HELP WITH DECLUTTERING.

www.flylady.com Flylady is the ultimate online clutter buddy. Join her mailing list to receive decluttering tips by e-mail.

www.tabithamiller.com/clutter.htm Visit Tabitha Miller's excellent Web site on decluttering classrooms.

www.loveathome.com/clutter.htm Debbie Williams presents practical ideas for helping children declutter at home, but the suggestions work equally well in the classroom.

✳ TRY THIS

Begin a decluttering campaign. Start with this time line and insert your own deadlines. Soon, your classroom will be clutter-free. Give yourself the satisfaction of checking off each action as it is completed. Or use some of the little motivational stickers you give the kids.

✔	DATE	ACTION	
		Prepare	Create a perfect-room album using catalogs, drawings, etc.
			Bring in one beautiful item to motivate your decluttering.
			Make a list of all the areas that need to be decluttered.
		Clean	Top of desk
			Desk drawers
			File cabinet top drawer
			File cabinet second drawer
			File cabinet third drawer
			File cabinet bottom drawer
			Storage closet
			Still working on storage closet
			Bookshelves
			More bookshelves
			Other shelves
			Window ledge
			Storage boxes
			More storage boxes
			Computer files
			More computer files
			Anything else that needs attention
		Celebrate!	Photograph your clutter-free classroom

7

INTERIOR
DECORATION

WHERE EAST MEETS WEST

The decorating colors and principles of feng shui are very basic and should be enhanced for use in an American classroom. As you arrange your posters, books, and accessories, continue to consult the bagua and its five elements. In this chapter, the traditional elements of design as accepted by interior designers will be integrated with the feng shui principles.

◎ Color

The feng shui color palette is rather plain compared to the interior decorator's color wheel. However, when you combine the logic used by the ancient Chinese feng shui practitioners with modern paint possibilities, you can incorporate the unlimited modern color palette that is so appealing to today's children.

The colors of the elements and their location on the bagua as they apply to your classroom orientation will be your first concern. Then consider accent colors—those colors that strengthen the main color but should be used only as highlights. In addition to considering the colors of the elements and their accent colors,

ELEMENT	COLOR OF ELEMENT	MODERN ADDITIONAL COLORS	ACCENT COLOR
Fire (S)	Red	Rust, salmon, peach, pink	Green
Earth (SW)	Yellow	Beige, brown, ochre	Red
Earth (NE)	Blue-green	Turquoise, teal	Red-orange
Earth (center)	Orange	Beige, ochre	Yellow or red
Metal (W)	Silver, gold, white	Bronze, aluminum	Turquoise or yellow
Metal (NW)	Silver	Charcoal gray	Orange or beige
Water (N)	Black	Navy blue	Gold, silver
Wood (E, SE)	Green	Olive, kelly	Blue or black

pay particular attention to the destructive cycles outlined in Chapter 5.

Look at the colors that you should use in each area of your room. Use either the Western style–orientation or the traditional compass orientation to determine where you should have specific colors.

Interior decorators use color to elicit certain feelings. The red, yellow, and orange combination helps people feel warm, as they are the colors of the south and southwest. However, they are also used as control colors in the northeast, southeast, and east to counterbalance the cold blue, purple, and green of those sectors.

Remember to consider the yin and yang when placing colors around the room. Yin colors are drab, dark, muted colors, while the yang colors are bright and alive. Dark, muted colors are very depressing, while yang colors are alive and inviting. It is good to have a balance of each throughout the room, not limiting them to one specific area, but balancing each other. For example, if you place a plant with a dark red flower in the south area of the room, that plant should have medium to light green leaves. Make sure those leaves stay nice and green by fertilizing at regular intervals.

When you give children awards such as balloons, consider each child's yin/yang personality when choosing the color, style, and message.

✎ GREAT IDEAS!

- Red increases restlessness and commands attention. Use sparingly in the recognition area.

THE PSYCHOLOGY OF COLOR

Color influences moods. Warm colors stimulate activity. Cool colors calm. Beyond those generalizations, specific colors with their accompanying tints and shades, elicit specific responses in students when used over large areas (Kicklighter and Kicklighter 1992).

- Orange has a similar effect to red, but is subtle, especially in its tints of peach and salmon. The lighter shades work well in the friendship corner.

- Yellow is sharply focused by the eye and is a cheerful color. Use it to target weekly themes and student achievement.

- Green reduces muscular tension and is good for concentration. It is great in any shade or tint in any area except earth.

- Blue makes it difficult to focus, and does not attract attention. In fact, blue light has been proven to retard the growth of plants. Blue is a poor choice for classroom wall color and if yours cannot be repainted, cover the walls extensively with color-appropriate posters. It is a very draining color.

- Purple is a combination of the active red and passive blue, and as such is a neutral, but pleasing, color. It disturbs eye focus slightly, so it should be used in very small areas that you want students to notice frequently.

- Black, white, and gray are emotionally neutral unless they are used in very large areas. If your walls are painted gray or white, consider covering them with fabric drapes or posters in bagua-friendly colors.

Until now, you have learned about solid colors. Feng shui also recognizes that patterns can have an impact on the environment.

Star and zigzag shapes attract attention. Certainly teachers have used this for a very long time, placing stars and arrows on anything they want the students to notice. Since these shapes are related to the fire element, highlight students' best work in the south, which, incidentally, is also the fame area of your room.

Vertical stripes harness the tree energy, a wood element, and encourage growth. They belong in the east and southeast. Place your growth charts—for both physical and mental growth—in this area.

Circles, dots, and spots belong in the metal areas, which is also your creativity area. Place lateral thinking puzzles in circles to stimulate interest.

Wavy, curved lines belong to the water element. They are calming and encourage tranquility. You may be tempted to place these all over the room, but be careful—the water energy symbol has no place in the south where fire controls that area.

So, what is all this information telling you about the placement of colors in your classroom? Consider the sample room on page 80, rotate it to coincide with your orientation, and place your colors accordingly. The section numbers correspond to the bagua areas.

The chi in a classroom is very sensitive to color. Accurate placement of colors according to the bagua will greatly influence student performance. The organization of colors in a regular sequence fosters organizational skills and calms the yang of so many young bodies in a room. Be careful to achieve a balance of shades (yang) and tints (yin) so the room is not overdone with either invigorating or calming influences. Although your objective may be to have a classroom of calm students who sit

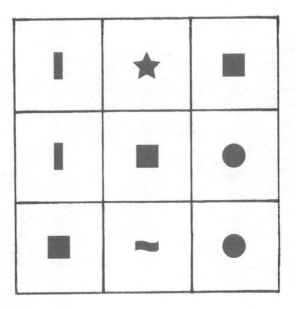

in their seats and never answer without raising a hand, too many yin colors may strangle the students' natural curiosity and stifle mental growth.

Windows

4	9	2
Plants with purple or red flowers would grow well in this corner. It is also a good place for your own storage.	This is a good place for the American flag. Add stars and arrows to posted student achievements.	Put a yellow happy face poster near the classroom rules. Post names of students who are good helpers.
3	**5**	**7**
Books arranged on a wooden bookshelf encourage their use. Use tall bookshelf to stimulate the wood element.	Place yellow messages of encouragement on desks. Avoid flower forms; use squares or stars.	A whiteboard surrounded by a metallic frame is perfect here. Place key words in circles.
8	**1**	**6**
This is the perfect corner for an aquarium. Keep goldfish in it to add the accent color. This is also a good location for your globe.	This career area would be good for posters related to occupations. Post due dates and homework assignments here.	Use a white or gray background for your travel posters. This is also a good corner for your computers.

Door

◎ Other Design Elements

Although color is a significant design element, other design principles, such as space, rhythm, emphasis, and balance, should also be part of your classroom design plan.

Space

Just as your living space may be divided into areas for watching television, reading, working at a computer, or dining, so, too, should a classroom be divided for specific tasks. For lower elementary classrooms where reading groups are an integral part of the curriculum, a section of the room is usually partitioned for this purpose. Consider using the southwest corner for this purpose. This area controls partnerships, so locating a reading group there would encourage interchange among students during discussion of the text. The northeast is the knowledge corner, so it also quite naturally serves as a reading area.

Set your reading corner apart in some way. Use a special "reading carpet" in colors that support the corner you have chosen. Both the northeast and southwest corners need squares supported by triangles. Trapezoid tables work well for that purpose. If you only have a round table, then perhaps you might locate your reading corner in the northwest diversity corner. Wherever you choose to place the reading corner, make sure your back is firmly placed against a wall, not a window. However, if that is your only option, use a Japanese-style screen behind you. This screen may also be used as a felt board if covered with a nappy fabric.

This was our counter-productive logo.

Consider your other spaces in the same way. A storage corner where papers, pencils, crayons, and markers are stored should also be set apart somehow. Color-code the storage bins according to the bagua recommendations, perhaps. Think about your northwest travel/diversity corner. Set it off from the rest of the room with a table (preferably round) draped in a multicultural fabric pattern. Remember to change your display frequently and wash the fabric occasionally.

Rhythm

This design element is achieved in a variety of ways: through repetition, graduation of sizes, and radiating patterns. Chi thrives on rhythm. Rhythm is easy to achieve through the use of a classroom theme. In the beginning of the year, help your students to find a theme. Avoid violent animals such as lions as they tend to elicit violent responses. Instead, focus on themes that encourage forward movement such as comets, trains, kites, and dolphins. Place pictures or silhouettes of your theme around the room, perhaps with spelling words or multiplication tables on them. You may decide to have a general circus theme, then use monthly subthemes of circus animals, clowns, and circus acts.

Emphasis

This is the center of attention in any room design. It could be your bulletin board with its brightly colored border and attention-grabbing arrows. It could be your multicultural corner with an African sculpture. Whatever you decide to have as your focal point, consider these three rules:

- ***The point of emphasis should dominate your room, not overpower it.*** Certainly this is an extreme example, but if you were to shine a bright spotlight on your computer area, the students will surely gravitate to the computers frequently. Likewise, having bright, yang colors only in one section of the room has the same effect as the spotlight.

- ***No other features in the room should compete with the focal point.*** The feng shui classroom is balanced in its use of color, texture, shape, and space. However, only one area of the room should shine as your focal point. Ask a few colleagues to walk into your newly decorated room and ask what they see first. If they give different answers, you know that you have multiple focal points. Adjust those extra areas that were mistakenly mentioned as your focal point to be slightly less eye-catching. Also, the most attractive corner should be in the bagua area that you most want to activate—perhaps knowledge, creativity, or diversity.

- ***Make sure your center of attention is where you actually want your student's attention.*** If you place colorful pieces of plastic removable shapes on your window, your students' attention will be directed there. If you have your center of attention over the blackboard or in the reading corner, your students will direct their primary attention to that area. Consider your priorities for your classroom when determining where you want your focal point.

Balance

Whether you are considering traditional interior design or feng shui, balance is an important part of any room. Without it, you feel as if one side of the room is visually heavier than the other side of the room. Formal balance, the placing of identical objects on either side of a central object, is usually impractical in a classroom. Consider instead, more informal balance by placing items of equal visual weight on both sides of a central point. For example, balance your long, low desk with a high, thin bookcase on the opposite side of the room. Balance the black chalkboard with a white or light-colored bulletin board background on the opposite wall. Remember yin and yang? If your room has too much of either, it will feel unbalanced. Chi loves a balanced classroom. It will swirl from one side of the room to the other as it energizes your students on the way.

Remember, if you don't feel comfortable in your classroom, it's a safe bet that your students don't feel comfortable, either. When you decorate and arrange your classroom, consider both feng shui and Western design principles. Certainly you could use only one or the other, but why not combine the best of both worlds?

When our choices in selecting and arranging our environments are focused on comfort and safety, and when we surround ourselves with the things that we love, we enhance the circulation of vital Ch'i. This approach creates our own personal paradise (Collins 1996, 55).

Look around your classroom. List the design elements you find in each area. Do they align with the bagua, or should you shift some of the posters and re-paper some of the bulletin boards? Create a chart like this (examples given):

AREA	COLOR	SHAPE	ELEMENT	KEEP	TRASH OR DONATE	MOVE TO
Recognition	Blue (child's poster)					Diversity (NW)
Diversity		Round (globe)		X		
Knowledge			Dead plant		Trash	

FENG SHUI for the HOME SCHOOL

The child who learns at home also benefits from the feng shui environment. His or her entire house becomes the classroom. However, for the purpose of this book, only the workspaces will be considered—the classroom area and the child's room.

◉ The Classroom Area

Assuming that you use a dining table for the home classroom, consider that each seat at the table carries with it a specific intention. Using the floor plan on page 89, place your children accordingly.

- The power seat for the parent/teacher is one that faces the door, yet is not directly opposite it. This seat should also be backed by a solid wall. While class is in session, if a door is located near the head of the table, it should remain closed. If this is not possible, a screen should be placed there to block outgoing flow of chi.

- Children who are likely to converse should be seated next to, rather than opposite, each other, at 1 and 2, or 3 and 4.

- An insecure child should sit in position 3, with his or her back to the wall between the parent/teacher and another child.

- A child striving for more independence, perhaps an adolescent, should sit at position 4, the seat with easiest access for exit, a symbol for his or her budding autonomy.

- The child most easily distracted should sit at seat 1 or 2 where he or she cannot see out the window.

- Sit confrontational children at positions 1 and 4, or 2 and 3.

- If you still don't have a good place to seat your children, go back to Chapter 2 and determine each child's optimum direction.

Remember to keep your instructional area as clutter-free as the rest of your house. Although it is tempting to pile the sup-

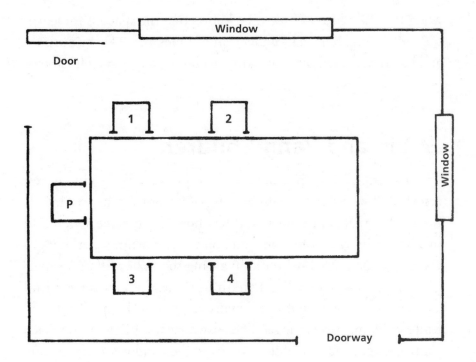

Door

Window

Window

P

1   2

3   4

Doorway

plies for each grade in a different corner, it is better feng shui to organize them neatly. Once again, consider the bagua. Each area is assigned a different number, so you can assign a specific area of the room for a specific grade level. Storage items need not be expensive. Simple shelving, organized and labeled, is enough to prevent clutter from accumulating if you set aside a "clutter-down" time at the end of each day.

Sounds are essential to the success of any classroom, but most particularly the home classroom. When the child uses a room for multiple purposes, it is important to designate the time and space by playing appropriate background music. For example,

As the child grows, her social and academic skills can be enhanced by her relationship with music. Music can mirror her half-understood emotions and help her learn to express what she feels. Making music with others can strengthen her bonds with her family and community and connect her to her cultural heritage. (Campbell 2000, 4)

when the child hears Mozart, he knows that the space is for learning, not eating. Sort your collection of tapes and CDs by purpose and you have added one more dimension to your home classroom.

Yin and Yang Children

As with any mix of people, some children will be yin (quiet, reserved, shy) and others will be yang (loud, boisterous, excitable). Remember that your objective is balance. If you place a yin child in a primarily yin room, you won't light any learning sparks. Conversely, if you put a yang child in a yang room, he will be so energetic, neither of you will get anything done. So, how do you find a balance in a room that will usually tend toward yin with its off-white walls and low ceilings? The answer again is in how you place your children. Face yin children toward the windows—lots of yang there between the natural sunlight and movement of birds and clouds. Face yang children toward the yin off-white wall where they will be less distracted by the world outside of their home.

In their individual rooms, you can stimulate the yin and yang children in different ways.

GREAT IDEAS!

If you have a yang child who needs a calming influence, use

- Soft lights (table lamps only)

- Muted colors (peach, pale green, blues, and earth tones)

- Padded furnishings

- Wall-to-wall carpet

- Soft, smooth textures

- Rounded corners

And if you have a yin child who needs gentle stimulation, use

- Bright colors (bold shades primary and secondary colors)

- Overhead and table lights

- Glossy finishes on the furniture

- Hardwood floors with area rugs

- Square corners

- Interesting textures (corduroy, gauze)

Two words of caution if you plan to redecorate your child's room: ask first. When you try to stimulate a yin child with yang

decorations, or calm the yang child with yin decorations, you will be going against the child's nature. It will be your challenge to introduce the yin/yang concept to your children and have them help you decide how and where to introduce the opposing forces to gain a balance in their rooms. Look to the bagua, as well, for assistance in where to place yin and yang elements. Remember, you can't have an all-yin or an all-yang room, or the room will become unbalanced. The occupant will bring his or her own energy into the room. The room needs to have some of that energy to make him or her feel welcomed, while having some of the opposing energy for balance.

◉ Your Child's Room

In addition to planning your child's room for yin and yang effects, consider placement of his or her belongings according to the bagua. Look at each area of the room, each piece of furniture, and each collection of possessions to determine optimum placement.

Knowledge—desk, computer, jigsaw puzzle, globe, open storage shelves; avoid plants

Family—books, plants, photographs of family; avoid computer, TV, and CD player

Possessions—collections of all kinds (stuffed animals, baseball cards, stamps, etc.), bank, dresser, closet; avoid computer, TV, and CD player

Recognition—awards, pets in cages, lamp; avoid aquariums and mirrors

Friendship—pictures of friends, table with two seats, games; avoid plants and CD players

Creativity—blocks and other creative play toys, art supplies, bed, computer, shiny things (such as jewelry); avoid pets in cages

Diversity—computer, CD player, TV, posters, doll house; avoid pets in cages, too much light

Careers—mobiles, aquarium, mirror, comfortable chair, floor lamp; avoid clay and especially avoid clutter in this area

Self—square or oval area rug in earthy colors; avoid clutter and plants

◉ Feng Shui Personalities

Just as it is important to understand each child's learning style, it is also important to learn each child's feng shui style. Your children will show tendencies toward one of the five elements. Those tendencies are both positive and negative. Each element is closely aligned to Howard Gardner's *Theory of Multiple Intelligences*. It is your duty to foster the positive characteristics while discouraging the negative characteristics by making use of each child's specific intelligence.

Families who have utilized simple feng shui principles have noticed improved health, more restful sleep, better study habits, reduced sibling rivalry, increased friendships, and general family harmony. (Olsen 2002, Web site)

ELEMENT	POSITIVE TRAITS	NEGATIVE TRAITS	LEARNING STYLES
Fire	Energetic, inquisitive	Easily distracted, hasty	Kinesthetic
Earth	Careful, cooperative	Shy, stubborn	Intrapersonal, existential
Metal	Thorough, serious, investigative	Obsessive, picky	Logical, musical
Water	Flexible, thoughtful, respectful	Secretive, emotional	Interpersonal, verbal
Wood	Flexible, thoughtful, respectful	Secretive, emotional	Interpersonal, verbal

Use your child's "intelligence" to expand his knowledge.

Teaching children at home requires creativity and structure on your part. You need to energize each child individually while teaching your family collectively. You can do this in many ways, but using feng shui to create an inviting environment for learning will make your task so much easier.

☺ Classroom Plants for Feng Shui

In his book, *How to Grow Fresh Air*, environmental engineer, Dr. Bill Wolverton (1997) explains about the beneficial ability of certain plants to remove toxins in the air. Feng shui appreciates the ability of anything that removes obstacles to the effective movement of chi, and certainly toxins would be included as one of these obstacles. During the 1980s, Wolverton found evidence that spider plants removed 95 percent of formaldehyde from the air in a sealed chamber during a twenty-four-hour period. Formaldehyde can be emitted from ceiling tiles, varnishes, and particleboard. It irritates mucus membranes and can cause dermatitis.

Now, drawing upon his research for NASA's "Sick Building Syndrome" research, Wolverton has identified other plants that have beneficial effects on the environment:

- Areca palm
- Lady palm
- Bamboo
- Rubber plant
- Dracaena
- Dwarf date palm
- Ficus
- Boston fern
- Peace lily
- Gerbera daisy
- Chrysanthemum
- Chinese evergreen

Wolverton recommends a mixture of plants in a room because different plants remove different toxins. He suggests two or three plants for every one hundred feet of floor space. Therefore, if you have a thirty by thirty foot classroom, you would need around twenty plants spaced around the room—except, of course, in the friendship and knowledge areas where woody plants are not recommended. In an average classroom, twenty or so plants might indicate that each student could take personal care of one plant.

Remember to water your plants frequently, but not so much that you encourage mold build-up. Horticulturalists prefer to water plants in a pot with a hole in the bottom, letting the water drain through into a sink, then returning the plant to a dry base. Spanish moss or aquarium gravel placed on the top of the soil will help keep the moisture in while discouraging the growth of

www.state.ma.us/dph/beha/IAQ/reports/
auburn/aubpes.pdf The complete text of the
Massachusetts Indoor Air Quality Assessment.

http://iaq.iuoe.org/iaq_htmlcode/iaq_news_
clips/Tough%20Atmosphere%20for%20
Learning.htm Synopsis of a similar study
conducted in Arizona.

mold on the top. Also, clean your leaves occasionally so they can do a thorough job of cleaning the air. A friend of mine uses a milky solution to clean the leaves of her plants: one-half cup of dry milk to one quart of water. The leaves have a healthy, shiny appearance when she is done. One exception is the African violet. They like to soak water from the bottom of the pot and never like to get their leaves wet. Dust their leaves by gently brushing them with a dry, camel-hair artist's brush. Finally, clean your pot exteriors with a mixture of one part bleach to ten parts water. This also discourages mold growth.

◎ Poisonous Plants

The following plants have been identified as poisonous and should be avoided where children are present.

Arrowhead	Delphinium
Azalea	Devil's ivy
Boston ivy	Dieffenbachia
Caladium	Elephant ear
Calla lily	English ivy
Castor bean	Euphorbia
China berry	Four o'clock
Daffodil	Foxglove
Death camas	Glory lily bulb

Hemlock holly berries

Hyacinth

Hydrangea

Iris

Jack-in-the-pulpit

Jerusalem

Cherry jimson weed

Jonquil

Lantana camara

Larkspur

Lily-of-the-valley

Lobelia

Mistletoe

Morning glory

Narcissus

Nephthytis

Night blooming jasmine

Nightshade

Pencil tree

Periwinkle

Philodendron

Pokeweed

Potato sprouts and leaves

Privet

Red angel's trumpet

Purging nut

Rhododendron

Rhubarb leaf

Rosary pea

Tobacco

Tomato vines

Wisteria

Yellow jasmine

Yellow oleander

Yew

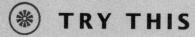 **TRY THIS**

In addition to the physical setup of your learning space, try other feng shui remedies to encourage learning:

1. Target an area of the learning room to energize—perhaps knowledge or creativity, depending on your needs.

2. Use aromatherapy to energize that area. Citrus rinds—lemon, orange, grapefruit, or tangerine—excite an area while creating a comforting, inviting aroma. Remember to replace them when they lose their scent. You could also place a lemon-scented plant such as lemon-scented geranium in any bagua areas that support plants. Be careful not to use lemon verbena as the pointed leaves could create poison arrows. Caution: Although many herbs and plants have been identified as having beneficial aromatherapy benefits, some of those plants have been identified as being poisonous. Check the list of poisonous plants on pages 96–97.

3. Add sound to liven the area. Use wind chimes or background music.

4. Add motion to attract attention to the focus area. Use mobiles, light airy objects such as feathers or silky fabrics over a vent, or a water fountain.

9

THE TEACHER at HOME

Just as your students come to school with "excess baggage" from their life at home, so do you. You come to school thinking about your mother who needs to go into a nursing home, your pending divorce, or your child who has just been diagnosed with juvenile diabetes. These events are part of your Man (or Woman) Luck and the only thing you can do is deal with each problem as it comes along. However, it is important that you give yourself a boost during these trying times by manipulating the Earth Luck of your home. Adjust the feng shui so your home supports your life rather than undermines it.

When you walk into your home, whether it is a house, an apartment, or a single room, it should say a hearty, "Welcome!" You should feel embraced by your surroundings, so that you can effectively deal with anything life throws your way. This is the essence of feng shui. The feng shui in your classroom is merely an extension of your home feng shui. The feng shui in your home will support your decisions and facilitate your career, relationships, financial situation, education, and travel interests. Feng shui at home is like lotion for dry skin or lubricant for squeaky door hinges. It helps your life go smoother.

Each area of your home needs special feng shui attention. Remember that the bagua and remedies that applied in the classroom will similarly relate to your living space. Also remember that the information contained in this book is a very basic approach to the feng shui of living spaces. Check out a feng shui reference book for more detailed information.

◉ Entrance

As you approach your home, what do you see? An overgrown mess of weeds in the front yard? A house with a stone façade, stone walkways, and a stone wall? Or perhaps you live in an apartment building with ten wooden doors in a row. Each of these scenarios indicates feng shui that needs adjustment. In the first example, there is too much clutter. In the second, there is too much of the earth element. And in the third, there is too much of the wood element. Feng shui remedies outlined in Chapter 5 will help with these and any other imbalances you may see.

For example, the overgrown yard is an easy fix. Get out there and toss the weeds, fertilize the lawn, and plant attractive flowers. Try these other simple remedies:

📌 GREAT IDEAS!

- Too much wood in the form of columns, wood doors in a row, or wood siding?

  Add a fire feature—perhaps red flowers.

  Paint your door red. Not only is red an outstanding feng shui color for the front door, it also "burns" the effect of too much wood.

- Too much earth in the form of bricks and stones?

  Contain the earth—place metal on either side of the door. Copper lanterns would be a good choice.

  Trees and shrubbery near the house weaken earth.

- Too much metal if you have aluminum siding?

  Add a water feature—blue, black, or gray shutters, perhaps.

  The red door works here, too, by melting the metal.

Watch out for poison arrows that are aimed directly at your home. Other buildings, which have corners that point directly at your home, are particularly dangerous. Deflect that chi with a fence, hedgerow, or even a bagua-shaped mirror.

CAUTION: Traditional feng shui practitioners recommend strongly against placing a bagua-shaped mirror inside of your home. It is very effective outside, but can be extremely ineffective inside.

With the stairs directly aligned to the front door, a strategically placed mirror will help reflect the chi back into the home.

The front door of your home or apartment is very important—it is the mouth of your chi. By controlling how chi enters your living space, the front door governs how difficult or easy your life will be.

Remember that much of feng shui is about symbolism. If you have a split-level house and immediately need to decide whether to go up or down, your life may be filled with difficult decisions. If, after you enter your home, you are confronted with a blank wall or, worse yet, a bathroom door, the chi will be stopped or flushed. Not a good situation.

Just as the front door is the entrance for chi, it can also be the exit for your chi. Having a front door at the end of a flight of steps is like letting your child ride a sled down the steps and out the front door—a very fast and very dangerous exit. You're not going to move your door or your steps, so what can you do? Go back to the remedies. Use a mirror to reflect the chi back into the house after it travels down the stairs.

Be careful that your front door does not directly face the back door or a large window, as that will effectively show your chi the best way out of your home. Everything, including chi, follows the path of least resistance. Create a few small obstacles for your chi between the front and back. A crystal in the window will definitely help because the chi will bounce happily back around the room following the rainbows.

Pay special attention to your entrance—the space that leads up to your door and the area directly behind your door. It is a powerful channel for chi. Your goal is to invite the chi into your home and hold it there in a swirling pattern, while at the same time discouraging the ssu chi from entering and collecting. This is a challenge that may require deep consideration into your home's external elements and associated remedies.

◉ Kitchen

Traditionally, the kitchen is the heart of a home. It is where you prepare meals, eat together as a family, and do a multitude of other tasks, from homework to paying bills. It is not surprising, then, that the kitchen requires extra special feng shui care.

Returning to traditional interior decorating, look at the four basic kitchen arrangements:

The galley kitchen allows chi to flow freely from one end to the other. Consider installing a bifold door at one end to block chi's exit.

The corridor kitchen also allows chi to speed by the food preparation area. Slow it down by placing ceiling lights at either end.

Be careful that the sink is not directly next to the stove in an *L-shaped kitchen* because that will tend to put out the fire. If that is the case, place a barrier of ceramic tiles between the sink and stove.

The *U-shaped* kitchen is the best arrangement, provided your back is not to the opening when you are at the stove.

The general guidelines for kitchen maintenance are simple: eliminate clutter and concentrate on sanitation. This is just good

Just as the door to your house is the mouth of chi, so too is your classroom door. Make it as appealing and inviting as possible.

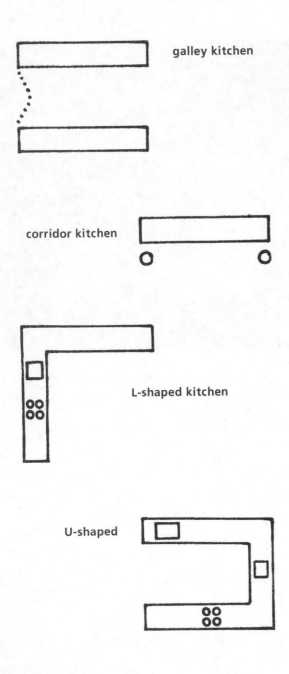

galley kitchen

corridor kitchen

L-shaped kitchen

U-shaped

common sense for safety in the kitchen. Feng shui adds these guidelines (Skinner 2001):

- The more stove burners there are in a kitchen, the happier chi is. To increase the number of burners, place a reflective surface behind them, creating the illusion that there are more.

- Be careful that you don't have a mirror facing the stove, as that will reduce the effect.

- The wood element supports the oven fire. Use green colors and plants to decorate.

- Although decorators use central islands for effect, these "blocks" tend to create an obstacle around which you and chi need to travel. If you have one, consider how many times you bumped into it on your way around the kitchen. Try to eliminate or move the island.

- Dried flowers, herbs, hot peppers, and any other hanging objects such as pots and pans may direct poison arrows at you while you cook. Relocate them.

- Pay attention to fast-moving shar chi and stagnant ssu chi, as neither will have a good effect on the quality of food prepared, which ultimately affects the health of the entire family. Use the remedies to slow fast chi and clear the clutter to move along stagnant chi.

- Use good lighting in the kitchen—natural and artificial. However, be careful not to locate a skylight directly over the stove, as it will drain the positive energies that the oven creates.

- Remember to look toward the bagua for help in arranging your kitchen. Place your ceramic dishes in one of the two earth corners. Pots and pans go well in the creativity area. Position your wooden kitchen table in the cooperation or friendship area.

Pay attention to things that tend to clutter so you can lessen common problems in the kitchen. Toss outdated spices—they lose flavor over time anyway. Remove trash at the end of each day. Clean up spills promptly. Recycle or donate cookbooks you no longer use. Consider the worth of each kitchen gadget. If you haven't used it in years, get rid of it. Remember, the kitchen is the heart of your home. When the kitchen is clean, organized, and safe, the rest of your home will surely follow.

◎ Bedrooms

The second most important room in your house is the bedroom. You spend one-third of your life there. The bedroom should be an inviting yin environment conducive to rest. If you have trouble sleeping, perhaps the introduction of a few feng shui treatments will eliminate some of your problems.

This bed captures all necessary feng shui features: balance, a firmly backed headboard, and posts that are not so high they are claustrophobic. Aside from the inevitable clock radios, no other electronic devices are near the bed.

The key to effective bedroom arrangement is balance. If you have too much furniture on one side of the room, or all the heavy pieces are in one area, your bedroom is unbalanced. Follow these guidelines for a feng shui bedroom (Skinner 2001):

📌 GREAT IDEAS!

- Your bed should be placed so you can see the door, but not directly opposite it. Your bed should also not be positioned between two windows or two doors, as this creates a draft for you and an escape route for your chi. And never, ever face your bed so your feet face the door—this is the mortuary position and is associated with much bad luck.

- The headboard should be against a wall that is not shared by a bathroom. It should also be higher than your footboard.

- Each side of your bed should be identical—place identical night stands and lamps at either side.

- Consider the view from your windows. If you have supporting trees, mountains, lake, or other beautiful, natural features, then by all means, bring that view into your room. However, if your bedroom windows look out onto the yard of a neighbor who has been a problem, then cover your windows with sheer curtains that let the light in, but shield the view.

- Under-bed boxes attract ssu chi. Keep the area beneath your bed free of clutter.

- Canopy beds can be extremely claustrophobic, trapping chi indefinitely. Instead of a heavy damask cover, use gauze or lace.

- Mirrors should not reflect the bed back to the door. This has the same effect as placing the bed so your feet face the door.

- Decorate your relationships corner carefully—it should be free of clutter and have two of everything you place there. Poor symbolism for this corner would be a picture of a single person or of two people looking away from each other. And certainly do not put a collection of stuffed animals in that corner because they may bring immature individuals into your life.

- Use yin colors—beige, amber, peach, and other earthy colors, especially for bed linens. Red solicits anger.

- If you have a missing corner, use an appropriate remedy. If you have a poison arrow, use an attractive screen.

- Electrical equipment has no place in the bedroom. Remove the television, computer, and electric blankets. Not only do they set up harmful electro-magnetic waves, they are also too yang for the bedroom.

Your bedroom should be your sanctuary—a place to get away from the stresses of everyday life, a place where you can relax and read or simply daydream. Does your bedroom say to you, "come, enjoy me"? If not, consider using some feng shui remedies.

Other Rooms in the House

Although the rest of the house is not as critical as the entrance, kitchen, and bedroom, they are important, nonetheless.

Dining Area

Most feng shui books treat the dining room as the primary gathering space for meals. However, in modern society, this area is now usually located in the kitchen. Therefore, my comments on this area will apply to whatever area you use for most of your meals.

The table should never be located directly under a toilet or washing machine. In some newer houses, architects place the laundry area on the second floor for ease in doing the laundry. However, this places a huge draining machine directly over some other critical area on the first floor. Fortunately for most of us, plumbers also have a say in the orientation of water features and most draining areas are generally located directly over each other.

The table should seat an even number of people, even if you have an uneven number of family members. Seat everyone according to the health direction (third location on the chart) as outlined at the end of Chapter 2, if possible.

The dining area should be a happy, yang area filled with the excited voices of people sharing their day, their hopes, their dreams, and disappointments. It should be decorated according to the bagua, perhaps with pictures of healthy food or gardens.

Living Room

Consider whatever room in which you congregate to watch television or simply relax as a family to be the living room. The formal living room of some homes is merely a showpiece where people seldom enter unless they are entertaining.

Be careful of the poison arrows created by heavy, exposed beams. Soften the effect by adding trailing vines along them or Chinese flutes to channel the chi back into the room.

Extremely high cathedral-style ceilings pull chi upwards without redirecting it downward. A ceiling fan that directs air downward is a good remedy (be careful—some ceiling fans can be set for either direction). Another solution that I have seen is the use of colorful flags suspended from the vaulted ceiling. If neither of these works for you, consider creating a "false" ceiling by adding a wall border eight feet from the floor.

Be careful of themes in your paintings—remember the symbolism. Angry or competitive animals create an angry or competitive mood. Serene scenes create a calm mood. Family portraits are wonderful. Place pictures of mountains behind the spot where you sit, and pictures of water in front.

Never place a mirror behind the sofa because it will provide little support for those who sit there. Similarly, never place the sofa under a window. And the television should energize the northwest corner.

The Home Office

The home office, whether it is a room or a designated area, is where you plan lessons, pay bills, and file the paperwork associated with life. You say all these things are not in one area of your home? Then pull them together—optimally in the southeast possessions area. Enhance that area with plants, flowers, and a water element. An excellent choice would be a fish tank, which combines water and fire (fish). Goldfish are wonderful—they are easy to care for and come in a beautiful variety of colors and shapes. Add one black fish to your tank for luck.

Clean up the files in your computer and elsewhere. I admit I am guilty of over-accumulation in this area. As a writer as well as a teacher, I am reluctant to toss something I may need to back up a future project. So, I offer you a word of advice: minimize. Look for duplication in your files, look for outdated files, and look for ways to organize whatever you can't bear to toss.

Orient the desk so you face your personal growth direction. You also need to see the door from your seat. You should face into the room rather than toward a wall and have a solid wall behind your seat. Just as in the bedroom, be careful of the view out the window.

Bathrooms

These rooms have special significance in feng shui because they are a strong source of water leaving your home. Remember the meaning of feng shui—wind and water? Chi travels along both channels. Obviously, you look to see how chi travels around your rooms, eliminating obstacles and blocking escape routes. Water will pull your chi out as well. Therefore, remember these guidelines regarding bathrooms (Skinner 2001):

📌 GREAT IDEAS!

- Always close the lid of the toilet when flushing. This is not only good feng shui, it is also a sanitary issue—particles from the toilet escape each time you flush, finding their way to your toothbrush, perhaps.

- The toilet should not be seen from the door. Sometimes this is not easy.

- Consider adding an "L" to counter space or using a screen to block the view.

- Since there is so very much water in the bathroom, control that element with earth features. Fortunately this is easily accomplished by using ceramic tiles.

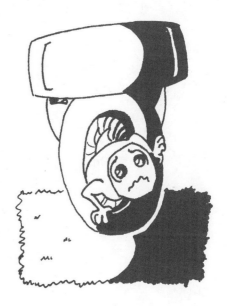

- Remove shower radios and other electrical devices from the bathroom. This is good feng shui and good safety.

- Keep the door closed or partially closed even when not in use.

All Other Areas

There are many other areas in the house that deserve your feng shui attention. Even the hallways can be feng shui compatible. My favorite hallway was in a student's house where I was tutoring. Her mother had chosen to place three small, beautiful crystal light fixtures along the long upstairs hallway. This lifted your spirits as you entered the hallway and gently distracted chi from traveling too quickly.

Steps should naturally be clear of clutter and should not be covered in red carpet as this captures the chi and will not allow it to go up or down. Bedroom doors should not directly face the steps. If this is the arrangement, add a wind chime or crystal to reflect the chi back into the bedroom.

By now, you probably see that there is not one area that escapes the fine-tuning that feng shui provides in your environment. At school, your classroom will be more organized and better suited for learning. At home, your rooms will support your life and help you to relax. There are even those who feel that your automobile and wardrobe are subject to feng shui guidelines. I'll leave that up to your own decision.

Feng shui is the key to success, happiness, and wealth. If you watch each area carefully for ways to improve the arrangement, your life will improve as well. When I first started feng shui, I was a skeptic, calling it hocus-pocus stuff that was a first cousin to magic illusions. Now I am a believer because I have seen the positive effects brought on by feng shui. Try feng shui—I know you will be pleased with the results.

When we do find that a critical challenge has apparently evoked a marked creative response, there is always the possibility that the response came not from people cornered by a challenge but from people who, in an exuberance of energy, went out in search of a challenge. (Hoffer 1963, 114)

TRY THIS

Lay the bagua over an outline of your house or apartment. Notice where each room is located. List the elements that predominate in each area, and then strive for a balance. Remember to use the supporting cycle if the element is weak where it should be strong and the reducing cycle where the element is strong where it should be weak. Then use the same process for each room. By doing this, you will be able to locate the areas in your home and in each room that are in most need of feng shui attention.

10
CONCLUSION

You're probably wondering how the author's classroom is decorated. Is it a perfect balance of feng shui and interior design elements? Absolutely not. My classroom, like yours, is a work in progress. I have no more time than you to sort files, rearrange furniture, and clean up old supplies. But I do have a head start because I started six years ago when I first discovered the power of feng shui. I try to keep my desk feng shui–compliant by cleaning the desktop at the end of every day. I also am fortunate enough to work in one of the few New Jersey schools to offer a floral design class. For a small fee, teachers can have a vase of fresh flowers delivered to their room each week. What a wonderful feng shui addition to our educational community! You can achieve the same benefit by placing a flowering potted plant on your desk.

THE IDEAL FENG SHUI CLASSROOM LAYOUT

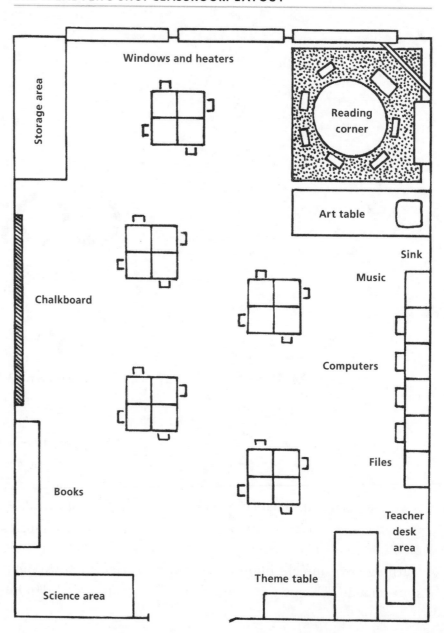

I refer to my room as an assembly of organized mayhem. Because I teach child development, I have toys instead of test tubes in my lab. I have children instead of chemicals. Unlike the chemicals, my lab subjects do not stay neatly in the cabinet until needed. Consequently, my decluttering activities need to occur more frequently than in other classrooms.

I have islands of feng shui in my classroom and in my home. I would like to have an entire continent, but in my busy life of teaching, writing, and maintaining a house, I find that I need to schedule activities to improve the feng shui. One of my favorite islands is a corner of my bedroom where I have placed a rocking chair. Prior to feng shui improvements, that corner was a sticky mass of chi lurking among boxes and clothes destined for Goodwill. Now I look at my corner every morning and breathe in the fresh chi that radiates from my completely feng shui friendly corner. One corner, one room, one house . . . one way in which I improved my life by implementing feng shui. There are other isolated islands of chi stimulators in my home, but that one area in my bedroom is my favorite.

When your home environment supports you, you will feel good all day long. When you feel good, you are more inclined to look for ways to improve other areas of your life. If you have a beautiful home but work in a classroom that has enough shar or ssu chi to frighten even the best feng shui master, your life will never be balanced. Balance is the key to success, happiness, and good fortune. Feng shui is the key to balance. Use it as I do to create harmony and balance in your classroom. Watch how your learning environment improves over time as you introduce feng shui remedies. Enjoy the benefits that it provides in all of your living and working spaces.

My favorite feng shui corner is in the wealth/possessions area of my bedroom. As such, I placed a wood rocker and table there. The cushion is a deep wine color. In the picture above the rocker are four columbine flowers in shades of red and purple. Naturally, the frame is rectangular. I needed to activate the chi there, so I chose a small lamp to brighten the corner and to add a touch of metal. A seagull on the driftwood sculpture adds the fire element. The quilted pillow is my own creation. It is made from a collection of ties my husband has worn through the years—naturally in shades of blue to introduce the water feature to this corner. Everything works together beautifully.

You can implement the findings of brain research, you can use new positive discipline measures, and you can use interactive computer programs related to your texts. However, without supporting all of these excellent educational tools with a learning environment that is organized and balanced would undermine your best efforts.

Your classroom should work like a well-oiled machine with all parts working together. If one of the gears is missing, dirty, or defective, the machine does not operate at optimum performance. Imagine your classroom without books, without paper, or without chairs. Certainly you could see the problems associated with these deficiencies. After you integrate feng shui remedies into your classroom, you will soon come to consider a room without feng shui to be similarly undersupplied.

Look around you. Where should you begin your classroom transformation? Make a list, develop a schedule, implement changes, and then chart your successes. Soon you will see an improvement in your classroom that you never thought possible. Feng shui works for me. It will work for you, too.

BIBLIOGRAPHY

Ayers, William. *To Teach: The Journey of a Teacher*. New York: Teachers College Press, 1993.

Brewer, Chris. *Music and Learning: Seven Ways to Use Music in the Classroom*. Tequesta, Florida: LifeSounds, 1995. Portions published on Web site www.newhorizons.org/strategies/arts/brewer.htm.

Brewer, Chris, and Don G. Campbell. *Rhythms of Learning: Creative Tools for Developing Lifelong Skills*. Chicago: Zephyr Press, 1991.

Brown, Simon. *Feng Shui for Business*. London: Ward Lock, 1998.

Campbell, Don. *Mozart Effect for Children*. New York: William Morrow. 2000.

Collins, Terah Kathryn. *The Western Guide to Feng Shui.* Carlsbad, California: Hay House, 1996.

Corrigan, Robert M. "Reducing Pest Problems in Schools by Reducing Clutter." *Pest Control Magazine.* 2001. Text available online at www.entm. purdue.edu/entomology/outreach/schoolipm/AI/PDF%20Files/Cutter5_9.pdf.

Finster-Bytnar, Elaine Jay. "Home and Office Feng Shui." www.fengshui-rockies.com/Home_Office.htm.

Gardner, H. *Frames of Mind: The Theory of Multiple Intelligences.* New York: Basic Books, 1993.

Hale, Gil. *The Practical Encyclopedia of Feng Shui.* London: Hermes House, 2001.

Hoffer, Eric. *The Ordeal of Change.* New York: Harper and Row, 1963.

Irlen, Helen. *Reading by the Colors.* New York: Perigree Books, 1991. Web site: http://www.irlen.com/index_sss.html.

Jones, Fred H. *Tools for Teaching.* Santa Cruz, California: Fredric H. Jones Associates, 2000. Web site: www.fredjones.com.

Kicklighter, Clois E., and Joan C. 1992. *Residential Housing.* South Holland, Illinois: Goodheart-Wilcox, 1992.

Kingston, Karen. *Clear Your Clutter with Feng Shui.* New York: Broadway Books, 1999.

Kirsch, Sandra. "Wind and Water as Business Builder." *Fortune Magazine.* August 10, 1992.

Klag, Prent, Ph.D. "Making Schools the Most Inviting Place in Town—The Disneyland Connection." International Alliance for Invitational Education. University of North Carolina at Greensboro, February 1995.

Lagatree, Kirsten M. *Feng Shui at Work.* New York: Villard Books, 1998.

Nelson, Mike. *Clutter Proof Your Business.* Franklin Lakes, New Jersey: Career Press, 2002.

Nelson, Mike. *Stop Clutter from Stealing Your Life.* Franklin Lakes, New Jersey: Career Press, 2001. Web site: www.clutterless.org.

NIEHS Kids Pages: www.niehs.nih.gov/kids/.

Olsen, Teri Ann Berg. "Feng Shui for Families." 2002.www.knowledge house.info.

Sacks, Sharon Z., Ph.D., and Rosanne K. Silberman, Ed.D., eds. *Educating Students Who Have Visual Impairments with Other Disabilitities.* Baltimore, Maryland: Brookes Publishing, 1999. Excerpted on www.pbrookes. com/store/books/sacks-2800/excerpt.htm.

Skinner, Stephen. *KISS Guide to Feng Shui.* New York: DK Publishing, Inc., 2001.

Too, Lillian. *Essential Feng Shui.* New York: Ballantine, 1998.

Wolverton, B.C., Ph.D. *How to Grow Fresh Air.* New York: Penguin Books, 1997.

INDEX

About the Author

RENÉE HEISS is currently a high school Child Development teacher at Northern Burlington County Regional High School in Columbus, New Jersey. In her twenty years of teaching experience, she has also taught Foods, Clothing, Interior Design, and seventh grade language arts. In 1997, she was named New Jersey Family Consumer Sciences Teacher of the Year. At local and state in-service meetings she has given workshops on Creativity, Anger Management, and, most recently, Feng Shui in Classrooms. She is a contributing author to *Crinkles Magazine* and has had many articles appear in regional parenting magazines and children's publications including *Highlights for Children*. Mrs. Heiss graduated from Douglass College in New Brunswick, New Jersey.

About the Illustrator

BRITTANY PLADEK is currently a student at Bryn Mawr College, majoring in English. She was the 2003 valedictorian at Northern Burlington County Regional High School in Columbus, New Jersey.